PANIC

Impending environmental catastrophe, threat of terrorism, viruses both biological and virtual, disease: there seem to be so many reasons to panic today. But what is panic and why does it happen?

This book uses a range of literature from sociology, cultural studies and popular psychology to develop an original analysis of panic in contemporary social life. Bringing together academic literature from a range of disciplines, films, novels and current affairs, it encourages thought about why and how we panic – both individually and collectively. Keith Tester explores how cataclysmic events and smaller-scale episodes expose the fragility of our relationships, institutions and expectations. He shows how thinking about panic reveals key aspects of contemporary social, cultural and personal relationships.

Panic is a highly readable and incisive introduction to the subject for students, scholars and all those who want to know what panic means and why it is important.

Keith Tester is Professor of Sociology at the University of Hull and is a Visiting Professor at the University of Leeds. This book builds on his research interests in the media, morality and critical cultural sociology. Previous books include *Humanitarianism and Modern Culture* (2010) and *Compassion, Morality and the Media* (2001).

SHORTCUTS – *'Little Books on Big Issues'*

Shortcuts is a major new series of concise, accessible introductions to some of the major issues of our times. The series is developed as an A to Z coverage of emergent or new social, cultural and political phenomena. Issues and topics covered range from Google to global finance, from climate change to the new capitalism, from Blogs to the future of books. Whilst the principal focus of *Shortcuts* is the relevance of current issues, topics, debates and thinkers to the social sciences and humanities, the books should also appeal to a wider audience seeking guidance on how to engage with today's leading social, political and philosophical debates.

Series Editor: Anthony Elliott is a social theorist, writer and Chair in the Department of Sociology at Flinders University, Australia. He is also Visiting Research Professor in the Department of Sociology at the Open University, UK, and Visiting Professor in the Department of Sociology at University College Dublin, Ireland. His writings have been published in 16 languages, and he has written widely on, amongst other topics, identity, globalization, society, celebrity and mobilities.

Titles in the series:

Confronting Climate Change
Constance Lever-Tracy

Feelings
Stephen Frosh

Suicide Bombings
Riaz Hassan

Web 2.0
Sam Han

Global Finance
Robert J. Holton

Freedom
Nick Stevenson

Planet Sport
Kath Woodward

Fat
Deborah Lupton

Reinvention
Anthony Elliott

Panic
Keith Tester

PANIC

Keith Tester

Routledge
Taylor & Francis Group
LONDON AND NEW YORK

First published 2013
by Routledge
2 Park Square, Milton Park, Abingdon, Oxon OX14 4RN

Simultaneously published in the USA and Canada
by Routledge
711 Third Avenue, New York, NY 10017

Routledge is an imprint of the Taylor & Francis Group, an informa business

© 2013 Keith Tester

The right of Keith Tester to be identified as author of this work has been asserted by him in accordance with sections 77 and 78 of the Copyright, Designs and Patents Act 1988.

All rights reserved. No part of this book may be reprinted or reproduced or utilized in any form or by any electronic, mechanical, or other means, now known or hereafter invented, including photocopying and recording, or in any information storage or retrieval system, without permission in writing from the publishers.

Trademark notice: Product or corporate names may be trademarks or registered trademarks, and are used only for identification and explanation without intent to infringe.

British Library Cataloguing in Publication Data
A catalogue record for this book is available from the British Library

Library of Congress Cataloging in Publication Data
Tester, Keith, 1960–
Panic / Keith Tester.
p. cm. – (Shortcuts)
Includes bibliographical references and index.
1. Panic – Social aspects. 2. Risk perception – Social aspects.
I. Title.
HM866.T47 2013
302'.17 – dc23   2012021941

ISBN: 978-0-415-63105-1 (hbk)
ISBN: 978-0-415-63106-8 (pbk)
ISBN: 978-0-203-09717-5 (ebk)

Typeset in Bembo
by Taylor & Francis Books

Printed and bound in Great Britain by
TJ International Ltd, Padstow, Cornwall

CONTENTS

Series editor's foreword		*viii*
	Introduction: what is panic?	1
1	Panic and risk	14
2	Panic and morality	39
3	Panic and trust	65
	Conclusion	90
Further reading, viewing and listening		*107*
Notes		*112*
References		*114*
Index		*118*

SERIES EDITOR'S FOREWORD

Anthony Elliott

Shortcuts is a major new series of concise, accessible introductions to some of the major issues of our times. The series is developed as an A to Z coverage of emergent or new social, cultural and political phenomena. Issues and topics covered range from food to fat, from climate change to suicide bombing, from love to zombies. Whilst the principal focus of **Shortcuts** is the relevance of current issues, topics and debates to the social sciences and humanities, the books should also appeal to a wider audience seeking guidance on how to engage with today's leading social, political and philosophical debates.

Written with extraordinary lucidity and insight, Keith Tester's examination of the force field of panic draws on sociological, political and cultural sources to unearth the complex interdependency of our lives in an age of advanced globalization. A society that is organized through complex networks of global interdependency is easily unnerved by panic – a state in which fear is lifted to the second power and which, ultimately, reveals the unmasterability of our lives. Tester explores the social and cultural factors that shape the conditions and consequences of panic in these early days of the twenty-first century, ranging from moral and media panics to the panic arising from global climate change. The book is an impassioned, sociological exposition of the contemporary age as a condition of panic, and presents to readers a vital shortcut on an issue of crucial public import.

INTRODUCTION

What is panic?

A while back my computer became infected with a virus. With growing alarm, increasingly loud cursing and a threat to throw the whole thing out of the window if it didn't start to behave, I watched with horror and amazement as folders became inaccessible and software stuck. My work, photographs and downloads were still there waiting to be used, but as time passed I could open fewer and fewer of them. Something was happening, some kind of catastrophe was unfolding and I could do absolutely nothing about it. I needed someone to blame.

First of all my anger was focused on computer hackers, who I castigated on the strength of no evidence at all as bored young men needing to get out of the house a bit more often. Then I managed to be a little more analytical and instead raged against capitalist exploiters. As I told myself, they deliberately create viruses to make people like me spend money on security software which is always about to become obsolete and is inevitably in need of expensive replacement. I've read newspaper stories about hackers, and I remember media coverage of the Millennium Bug: evidently all computers were going to stop at the first stroke of the year 2000 because of a fault in the design of software. Refrigerators in supermarkets were all going to fail, ruining the frozen food and creating shortages. Complex supply networks were all in danger of disintegrating. Consequently it was necessary to buy everything early, *just in case*. Apparently even nuclear power stations were at risk of explosion because their computer systems might malfunction. The only way the Millennium Bug could be fixed was – you've guessed it – by contracting very busy and therefore high-fee software consultants to resolve the problem, or by purchasing special programs from shops needing new footfall after the Christmas retail frenzy. Alternatively you could just take the risk and wait to see. Unsurprisingly when computers ticked over to the year 2000 nothing untoward happened at all. Even computers and systems that had not been 'fixed' carried on working as usual.

So thanks to the media I knew both hackers and capitalist software designers were blameworthy and dangerous to innocents such as myself. Yet the experience of the virus means I am not as innocent as I was. I take more care. I make sure everything is backed up, make sure I've got firewalls and anti-virus software to keep the hackers and fraudsters at bay. But I know they are still out there, and I reckon they will catch me again even though I have no idea when or how – will I even know *if* they have caught me?

I guess my feelings turning on my computer nowadays can be identified as a kind of low-level *fear*.

> "Fear" is the name we give to our *uncertainty*: to our *ignorance* of the threat and of what is to be *done* – what can and what can't be – to stop it in its tracks – or to fight back if stopping it is beyond our power.
>
> (Bauman 2006: 2)

According to Zygmunt Bauman, fear is one of the defining traits of our time, and what he calls 'liquid modernity' is the contemporary way of trying to live with it. We try to live with fear through our own resources, as individuals. On the one hand we make fear routine and just another of the many things with which we need to cope. On the other hand we rely on our own individual abilities to escape from the cause of the fear or to buy the solution from the experts. This is exactly what I did when my computer became infected. Simply by downloading antivirus software along with anti-spyware and other things which, to be perfectly honest, I don't understand but know I need (because I've read the relevant pages on the Internet) I tried to make my computer routinely secure from the dangers out there. I can do nothing about the threats themselves, and it never crossed my mind to work with others to stop the hackers and capitalists, but I have made myself as safe as I can be. The low-level fear is permanent but predictable and therefore itself a kind of routine. Nowadays I even give advice when friends tell me about the infections of their computers. They treat me as an expert because I have remained safe, even though I do not really know what I'm talking about. Actually I am both uncertain and ignorant. I'm also a little fearful.

But there is another strand to be pulled out of the mundane little story of my computer infection. If Bauman is right I can live with fear, but when I watched my computer slowly freeze my reaction was anything but routine. I wasn't at all uncertain or ignorant. I knew full well what was happening to my computer and therefore to a couple of years of work and files. This wasn't just worrying, it was disastrous. I knew for a fact there was nothing I could do about it. I was more than fearful. *I was in a panic.* The threat to throw the computer out of the window was nothing more than an attempt to run away, escape, from what was all too inevitable. The fear only came *after* the panic. This is the point at which the story of my computer becomes significantly more than a personal anecdote.

Panic, I propose, is an *unusual but typical* experience of the contemporary social situation. It is *unusual* because it is the effect of single catastrophic causal events. Yet panic is *typical* because single catastrophic events happen increasingly often – and indeed are increasingly catastrophic – because of the fragility of complex social relationships. Natural catastrophes like earthquakes, tsunamis and maybe even climate change do not cause panic because they are in themselves worse or more frequent than ever before, but because they are more able to demolish the social relationships that are fragile precisely because they are so complex.

This book is about panic. It has been written because: first, I believe panic is an important phenomenon which shadows our lives nowadays; second, how we panic and who we blame for the catastrophe is a way of pinpointing the most fragile aspects of contemporary social relationships; third, because if we can think about and with panic as a phenomenon we might be able to do something more than panic in the face of catastrophe. Of course, it's another matter entirely whether the alternative to panic is any more useful than a variation on the theme of throwing the computer out of the window.

In this Introduction I will, next, quickly survey the most important social scientific contribution to the study of panic in order to move towards the firm definition on which the rest of the book will be based. Second, I will put this definition into sociological perspective. I've already referred to the complexity of social relationships on a couple of occasions, but what does this mean? In what does the complexity consist? Third, and by way of conclusion, I'll offer the hypothesis that the book will explore. I'll also outline how the exploration will proceed.

What is panic?

Neil Smelser offers the classic social scientific definition of panic. He said it is, '*a collective flight based on a hysterical belief.* Having accepted a belief about some generalized threat, people flee from established patterns of social interaction in order to preserve life, property, or power from that threat' (Smelser 1962: 131; original emphasis). Something needs to be stressed about this definition, because it shapes how Smelser understands the causes and character of panic. He sees it as *a form of collective behaviour and not as an individual trait*. In other words for Smelser panic is sociological and not psychological. Smelser's definition of panic opens up a research agenda.

First of all, if panic is a 'collective flight based on a hysterical belief', there has to be a means of the communication of the belief. As Smelser puts it: 'Panic can only occur if information, opinions, and emotional states can be communicated from one potential participant to another' (Smelser 1962: 139). Smelser seems to assume communication happens because people are in the same situation. One of the examples he gives to illustrate this point is of soldiers on a battlefield. But of course this stress on communication also opens up the question of the media. Smelser himself didn't take the question of the media much further than a passing reference to situations in which, 'when telephone and radio service – as well as face-to-face contact – are restricted, panic may be reduced' (Smelser 1962: 139). There is much more to be said about the media than this, however. As later analysts like Stanley Cohen saw, collective belief in contemporary social relationships is indebted to the media much more than to immediately shared experiences (Cohen 2002). Furthermore, mediated communication cannot necessarily be collapsed into the same analytical frame as face-to-face contact.

Second, for Smelser panic is caused by 'belief about a generalized threat'. The threat must represent a catastrophic *strain* on 'established patterns of social interaction'. Smelser clarified what 'strain' means in this context: 'Some kinds of strain lie at least partially beyond human control. These include the ravages of storms, floods, and earthquakes. Besides these threats of nature, man faces dangers and uncertainties that vary according to the mode of institutionalization' (Smelser 1962: 135). The tsunami in Japan in 2011 is an instance of a natural strain. Meanwhile, by way of example, Smelser says panic about unemployment is softened because the institutionalization of benefits has reduced the strain of poverty caused by the lack of paid work. This point makes it possible to understand the panic caused by the banking crisis which broke out in 2008. The panic reflects the extent to which market deregulation in the 1980s and 1990s transformed the 'established patterns of social interaction' of banking institutions, and instead allowed them to operate in the conditions of profit-rich uncertainty called 'deregulation' which were legitimated by reference to the neo-liberal idol of 'market freedom'.

Third, if panic is 'collective flight' then, quite simply, there must be somewhere to which to flee. But the escape routes are made uncertain by the 'generalized threat'. Smelser said panic is impossible if escape routes are believed to be open, and indeed it is also impossible if escape routes are believed to be shut. In the first instance there is no panic because there is a widespread belief in the ability of everyone to escape the threat. In other words, there is no panic because everyone is believed to be able simply to flee. In the second instance there is no panic because if all routes are closed the threat cannot be escaped. There might be anxiety and terror, but this does not constitute panic because, as Smelser's definition establishes, panic means 'collective flight'. So by virtue of the definition if there can be no flight there can be no panic. Consequently: 'Panic is possible only when exits are defined as limited and possibly closing' (Smelser 1962: 137). For an example to illustrate this claim, Smelser points to the case of people blocking escape routes when a building is burning. They are all panicking because they believe their chances of escape are being rapidly reduced. If they could all get out easily there would be no panic, and similarly if they all believed they were stuck in the burning building they would not panic either. In the latter case they would just be terrified.

This example of people fleeing a burning building highlights one of the problems with Smelser's approach. He identifies panic with what he calls a 'hysterical belief'. Now, with the reference to hysteria Smelser was probably simply trying to point to the extreme emotions involved in panic, but the word carries baggage. To call something hysterical is to imply an irrationality about it. Here then, Smelser was probably trying to slip in some normative assumptions about the rationality of the 'established patterns of social interaction', and he probably sought to do this because of his theoretical presuppositions (which were indebted to Parsonian functionalism). However the example of the burning building is not at all irrational. To try to flee a burning building is actually a very sensible thing to do. Indeed empirical research on panic situations has shown how crowds trying to escape rarely behave irrationally and furthermore are rarely hysterical in any sense of the term. Despite what Smelser might lead us to expect, panicking crowds often consist of individuals who seek to cooperate with one another (Quarantelli 2001: 9). Contrary to Smelser's definition panic does not necessarily involve flight from 'established patterns of social interaction'.

Smelser tried to develop a concept of panic that could be used to direct and underpin empirical research. To some extent he succeeded, but his victory might well have been rather pyrrhic. Evidently few of the studies his work inspired actually confirmed his definition of panic. Indeed after around 50 years of work on social scientific approaches to panic Quarantelli was moved to wonder if, 'there is still any scientific justification for the continuing use of the concept in any technical sense ... [I]t is possible that the concept of panic within collective behavior in sociology may disappear as a technical term in the future' (Quarantelli 2001: 11).

Social science has problems answering the question 'What is panic?'. The most ambitious and insightful attempt to provide a definition which might be taken up and used by others rather seems to fail by the findings of the very research it inspires.

But whatever the definitional troubles of social scientists, people *do* panic. Perhaps if it is possible to understand why people panic it will then be possible to offer a more flexible definition than Smelser, a definition that is concerned less with internal rigour than with interpretative possibility. To do this it is necessary to understand the social relationships in which people panic, and indeed which make panic seem to be a plausible way of dealing with catastrophic events. The relationships are marked by the fragility of *complexity*.

On this basis I shall define panic as: *confrontation with the fragility of the complexity upon which daily routine is dependent*. The confrontation is an effect of a causal event.

What is complexity?

An initial insight into the meaning of complexity is provided by the story of my computer. Of course a computer is a highly complicated piece of equipment, but more significantly it is also *socially* complex. Each part of a computer is made separately, often in different countries, each part has its own resource requirements (minerals, plastics), and each has to be shipped to a central factory for assembly. Once it has been put together the computer has to be delivered to retail outlets. If one link in this chain were to fail, the process taking the computer from raw materials in different countries to my office would stop. One of the routine activities of my daily life is therefore entirely dependent on complex social relationships. Actually, all of my routine activities are dependent on relationships with and of others. After all I do not make my own clothes, grow my own food and neither did I build my own house.

I could not do any of these things even if I wanted. I lack the skills. Like you I am the subject of a division of labour in which my abilities are specialized. Durkheim made this insight one of the foundation stones of sociology, when he identified contemporary society as typified by *organic solidarity* (Durkheim 1984).

We all perform different specialized roles in the division of labour, and we come together on the basis of mutual dependency. We are *interdependent*. None of us is self-sufficient and able to sustain our own existence without the help of others. Norbert Elias put the point very strongly. He said: 'There is no one who is not and has never been interwoven into a network of people' (Elias 1978: 128).

Elias sought to make analysis of these networks the subject matter of sociology. He did this by looking at them through the concept of *figurations*. By way of example Elias mentions a game of cards: 'If four people sit around a table and play a game of cards together, they form a figuration. Their actions are interdependent' (Elias 1978: 130). There is no card game independently of the players, and the game only continues all the time they stay within the figuration. The success of the game is a result of their interdependency. Yet this interdependency is extremely complex. First it presupposes a shared and agreed knowledge of the rules of the game. This knowledge has to come before the game. Without the prior agreement the game would not be possible. The rules must be taken for granted and accepted as 'the way things are'. Second the performance of the game is a process in which the power is shifting from one player to another. It's not static. The relationships within a figuration are always in process of change. For Elias figurations of mutual interdependency can be found in all social relationships, ranging from a card game as in this example, to the largest networks: 'But the inhabitants of a village, a city or a nation also form figurations, although in this instance the figurations cannot be perceived directly because the chains of interdependence which link people together are longer and more differentiated' (Elias 1978: 131). Consequently the complexity of a figuration has many dimensions. It is *quantitative* in as much as figurations, like cities (and Elias's approach can be easily extended to global networks; Rohloff 2011), involve increasing numbers of social actors; second the complexity is *qualitative* because the interdependent actors take on increasingly specialized roles (and thereby become involved in processes of deepening interdependency); third the complexity is implicated in *space and time* in as much as the networks of interdependency can stretch far beyond the situation of any specific individual.

The networks of interdependency are consolidated through institutionalization. This consolidation in its turn structures the possibilities of the power struggles within figurations. Moreover, it becomes the precondition of routine social relationships. The consolidation is naturalized when the networks of interdependency are taken entirely for granted and accepted as the way 'things must be', as the order of things for which 'there is no alternative'. Consolidation leads to certainty, and to confidence in the reproducibility of the networks of interdependency. Consolidation hides fragility.

However, the certainties generated by the consolidation of interdependency are challenged by interdependency itself. Precisely as interdependency becomes increasingly complex it becomes more and more fragile. This is because the maintenance and reproduction of the network depends on the coordinated action of ever-more specialized individuals. Zygmunt Bauman gestures towards this point when he takes up Elias's word 'figuration' and defines it as, 'a non-random assembly of actors locked together in a web of *mutual dependency* (dependency being a state in which the probability that the action will be undertaken and the chance of its success change in relation to what other actors are, or do, or may do)' (Bauman 1990: 7). The withdrawal of one actor (whether an individual actor, specialized group in the division of labour, institution or nation) from a figuration radically decreases the likelihood of the maintenance of the network of interdependency, if not indeed actually makes its reproduction quite impossible.

There are two dominant reasons for the withdrawal of an actor from networks of interdependency. The first reason is the *risk event*. These events are linked to failures of technology or the consequences of natural disasters. But it is necessary to be quite clear here. A risk event is catastrophic on account of its impact on interdependency, not because of its own magnitude. This point especially applies to natural disasters. A volcanic eruption in Antarctica is of massively less *sociological* significance than a much smaller eruption in, say, Iceland. This is because an eruption in Antarctica makes few, if any, networks of interdependency fragile. But when Iceland's Eyjafjallajökull volcano erupted in April 2010 most north European countries closed their airspace for five days because of a panic about ash clogging up jet engines. The travel plans of around 10 million passengers were disrupted, and according to one estimate the airline industry lost £2.1 billion (Batty 2010).

Second, there can be withdrawal because of a *disorderly social event*. Here the networks of interdependency are made fragile because of the actual or amplified actions of groups which are identified as outside of a figuration and therefore as a threat to order on account of their *lack* of dependency. Their actions cause withdrawal on the part of those who are within the networks of interdependency because continued participation is taken to be dangerous. These groups are Cohen's folk devils (Cohen 2002). I was turning computer hackers into folk devils when I condemned them for their attack on the routines that I take completely for granted. Folk devils become an increasing focus of attention, and are invested with ever greater ability to make all things fragile, because even as they are excluded – and understood as excluding themselves – from the networks of interdependency, they give a human face to complexity and its problems. They *personalize* networks which stretch beyond persons. Furthermore, emphasizing folk devils means externalizing the blame and responsibility for panic. Folk devils absolve the routine and make institutionalization the answer.

Consequently, if panic is defined as *confrontation with the fragility of the complexity upon which daily routine is dependent*, it is now possible to clarify some of the implications of this definition:

First: confrontation is caused by a causal event of risk or disorder;
Second: contemporary social relationships are typified by networks of interdependency which are, on account of their complexity, fragile;
Third: routine daily life is predicated on the consolidation and naturalization of networks of interdependency;
Fourth: the causal event reveals the fragility of the consolidated networks.

This definition has the benefit of clarifying the difference between fear and panic:

> Fear is the *possibility* fragility *might be* revealed. Panic is the *certainty* fragility *has been* revealed. Fear suggests an existential condition of anticipation, whereas panic suggests a condition of crisis.

Conclusion

Building on the definition of panic which is offered above, this book explores the following hypothesis:

> *The confrontation with fragility is the sociological cause of panic.*

I'm less concerned with reaching a final assessment of the validity of this hypothesis than with offering some resources by which it might be thought through and debated.

The exploration has three main aspects. Chapter 1 looks at risk events, and it links panic to sociological theories about risk society. Chapter 2 concentrates on disorderly social events. This chapter examines moral panics, but I hope in a way that adds something to the debate rather than just covers what has too often become a rather regurgitative affair. Chapter 3 takes the debate away from risk and moral panic, and towards the personal, the ontological. This chapter considers personal panic, such as the fear of flying, and relates it to questions of trust and popular psychology. The Conclusion reflects on the preceding discussion but also tries to take it forward. It draws out an explanation of the kind of social self – the kind of character – who panics, and then tries to explore the political implications of panic. The book has been written in the spirit of trying to encourage thought and discussion about panic. Maybe thought and discussion are good first steps towards not panicking and acting morally and humanly instead.

I'd like to end this Introduction on a personal note, and thank the people who have given me the chance to write this little book, and those who have helped me. Anthony Elliott originally suggested the idea to me, and he has been a superb series editor – generous, supportive and committed. He is a proper intellectual, one of a dying breed. I am also grateful to Linda and Maddy Tester for all of their support, encouragement, good humour and distraction.

1
PANIC AND RISK

On Friday 11 March 2011 one of the most powerful earthquakes ever recorded happened off the east coast of Japan. The quake generated a tsunami which caused massive destruction when it hit land. Notwithstanding the stories of survivors and the footage of the unimaginable power of the tsunami sweeping all before it, attention quickly focused on the major damage caused to the Fukushima nuclear power plant. The cooling systems failed, the nuclear fuel rods overheated, and there were explosions and radiation leakages. Three of the reactors at the plant went into meltdown and the situation was not stabilized until December 2011, some nine months later. All of this was covered extensively on global television, making it a truly world event.

It was able to be a *world* event because it happened in Japan and, more significantly, not so very far relatively from Tokyo. In a straight line Fukushima is around 150 miles (about 240 kilometres) north of the capital. Yet this isn't a point about geography. Thanks to visual culture, business, tourism, technology, finance and personal relationships, Japan, and especially

Tokyo, is deeply woven into the networks of contemporary interdependency. It is very familiar as a world city because it is one of the places that make everyday routine lives possible.[1] The radiation leakage from Fukushima was so worrying precisely because it forced confrontation with the fragility of routine daily life, not just in Tokyo, nor Japan, but thanks to interdependency to some degree or another *everywhere*. Furthermore because the extent of the damage of Fukushima forced this particular confrontation it caused *panic*. This was because the air itself had supposedly become dangerous. Evidently even to do a routine activity like breathe would soon become lethal.

The evidence of panic is provided by the attempt of so many people to get out of Tokyo. By Wednesday 16 March many European expatriates were following the advice of their governments and actively seeking places on the next flight out. Radiation levels in Tokyo were ten times their normal level. There was increasing concern about the wind blowing even more radiation from Fukushima to the Tokyo area. Additionally the tsunami and earthquake had damaged the transport infrastructure. There could be no guarantees about the availability of food for those who stayed, and the escape routes were closing for those who were trying to get out. The British journalist Andrew Gilligan was near Fukushima itself when the disaster happened, and he reported on the crowds gathering at the local railway station:

> The railway station at Nasushiobara, the last one still operating near Japan's nuclear crisis area, was jammed with frightened people. In this ghost town of closed shops and offices, pedestrian-free pavements, and empty petrol pumps, the station was the only place still alive, and the only escape route that most had left.
>
> *(Gilligan 2011)*

But when these people from close to Fukushima arrived at Tokyo, they would have found just more cause for alarm.

Some people were fleeing from there too. France was at the front of the evacuation telling any of its citizens who had no great reason to be in Tokyo to leave 'for a few days'. Special flights to Paris were arranged due to demand. This was not surprising since it seems it was a French bulletin that triggered the attempts to flee the city. Evidently the French Embassy website had earlier said a 'radioactive wind' was heading for the capital. The Italian government and Alitalia were discussing arrangements for extra flights in and out of Tokyo, international businesses were hiring private planes to get their staff out of Japan (more likely it was just their top staff; evidently bankers were the first to run), and in Russia flights from the east to Moscow were sold out. The Turkish authorities told their citizens to avoid Japan altogether (Allen 2011; McCurry and Booth 2011).

Queues at the airports and railway stations rapidly became longer. Roads were blocked with traffic jams and shops were cleared by panic purchasing. All of this is exactly what Neil Smelser's definition of panic would lead us to expect. People were panicking to flee from a situation in which the escape routes were open at the moment but were believed to be beginning to close. As one Chinese student told British journalist Nick Allen at Narita airport: 'I heard a report that a nuclear rain was going to reach Tokyo in 10 hours so I just came straight here' (Allen 2011). The attempted flight was caused by belief in the likelihood of a 'radioactive wind' blowing over Tokyo. Such a belief is typical of one of the key strands of panic according to Smelser: 'A particular kind of *belief* must be present in order for panic to occur ... This belief has a generalized component (anxiety) and a specific or short-circuited component (fear)'. The anxiety becomes fear because of what Smelser calls a 'precipitating event' which offers the evidence justifying the panic. There is then the *'mobilization for flight'* (Smelser 1962: 133). The actions of the French authorities illustrate Smelser's account perfectly. First of all the announcement of the impending wind turned the generalized anxiety (radiation *could* pollute Tokyo) into fear (radiation *probably will* pollute Tokyo), and when the French authorities told their citizens to leave 'for a few days' they provided the precipitating event for escape attempts (radiation is *about to* pollute Tokyo). Furthermore by organizing special planes for French citizens, the authorities exacerbated mobilization for flight. After all if the French were being given the chance to leave, perhaps we ought to get out as soon as possible too. In this way the attempt to flee Tokyo fits another aspect of Smelser's definition of panic. It was a *collective flight*.

But for Smelser the collective flight of panic also implies a flight from 'established patterns of social interaction'. Now in one regard the Tokyo evacuation fits with this definition because, obviously, those who were trying to flee were necessarily abandoning their homes, jobs and indeed other people. They were abandoning their established patterns of interaction. To try to flee is precisely *not* an established pattern of interaction, and indeed social life would be completely impossible if flight were established as 'normal'. But the similarity of what happened in Tokyo to Smelser's definition breaks down. This is because people tried to flee Tokyo in what was actually a very orderly way. Smelser's definition implies a mad rush and crush for the exit, but this is not what happened. Yes a lot of people were trying to flee at the same time, but they did so according to what were in effect rather 'established patterns of social interaction'. Andrew Gilligan gives a good example in his story about getting away from Fukushima. He managed to get to the local train station. This is what he found:

> Inside the booking hall, there was Japanese-style panic – whose symptoms are not the same as those of Western-style panic. Even without the shouting and fighting, people were clearly under great strain. Many had flared nostrils and terrified eyes.
>
> *(Gilligan 2011)*

Of course this passage might not be entirely reliable – it seems to be more than a little indebted to stereotypes – but two interesting nuggets are contained within what Gilligan writes. First, the panic on the part of the people trying to get to Tokyo was actually orderly and within social norms and expectations. It was not of the sort that Smelser seems to imagine. Second, even if the content of Gilligan's observation is slightly questionable, it nevertheless raises an interesting question as to whether there are *cultural differences* in *how* people panic.

It's worth teasing out this last point a little. If there are cultural differences, then any biological explanations of panic can only be partial. Panic might well involve definite chemical reactions in the human body, but this does not of itself mean everyone panics in the same way. Indeed the chemical reactions can only happen because the person defines themselves as being in a situation where panic is appropriate. It is quite reasonable to postulate cultural differences in the ways of panic, so what makes the difference? The answer to this question comes from the networks of interdependency and how they have naturalized certain kinds of social character. The naturalization is due to the consolidation of routine through institutionalization. Certain character traits seem to be natural and intrinsic to 'people like us' because they have have been consolidated along with the networks of interdependency. These networks are not just laid on top of pre-existing social relationships, and they do not just force the pre-existent into the necessary mould. They are influenced in their social character formations by the specific social context in which they emerge. This context is shaped by the specificities of culture. Think of rose bushes. The form and vibrancy of the flowers will be different dependent on the soil in which they are planted and which provides the nutrients for their emergence. Consequently the character traits implicated in networks of interdependency will vary according to the conditions in which the networks emerge and are institutionalized. There is an interplay between network and character, and panic is the result of the interplay collapsing. We stop being able to know who and where we are.

In these terms it is possible to make a suggestion. When panic causes flight, it also causes escape to definite locations. These are the locations in which the interplay of character and interdependency might be reconfirmed through routine. By this argument airports and railway stations are not just *actual* departure points. They are also *symbolic* institutions in which it is possible to engage in routine behaviour of flight from here (such as buying a ticket or queuing even in times of panic). This explains an anecdote Gilligan gave about something he saw at the railway station close to Fukushima:

> A quarrel broke out in the ticket queue when one man tried to pay by credit card, holding everybody up. But there still was a ticket queue, and a queue to board [the train], even though it was about half a mile long.
> *(Gilligan 2011)*

This symbolic aspect of airports and railway stations is further illustrated by Steven Spielberg's 2004 film *The Terminal*. It is a comedy-drama about a refugee from a war-torn state who loses his papers at JFK in New York, and is consequently unable to leave. As a result he has to start living in the airport. The comedy comes from the concept of being stuck in a place which is all about movement, of being a resident in a transit place.[2]

But to return to Japan. Of course the panic was exacerbated by the erstwhile nature of the precipitating event, and specifically its *invisibility*. As one interviewee for a British newspaper put it: '"I'm not that worried about another earthquake – it's the radiation that scares me," said Masashi Yoshida, who was waiting for a flight out of Haneda airport with his five-year-old daughter' (McCurry 2011). A teacher told Andrew Gilligan: 'The problem with radiation is that you cannot know anything' (Gilligan 2011). And a mother told Nick Allen: 'It is windy today, and if the wind comes south the fallout will reach Tokyo. We have to get out. My friends are all worried too and many of them are also leaving' (Allen 2011). When people start talking like this, the social scientific antennae start to twitch, because what they are saying brings to mind the theme of *risk society*.

In this chapter we will explore the issue of risk society and panic. In the first section we'll set up an explanation of the Tokyo panic from within risk society theory, but we'll point to a problem – risk society theory says curiously little in any developed way about the media. Yet the media have to be central to the communication of risk because, as in our case, the risk is actually invisible. So, the second part of the chapter will look at the media. But the media are no longer a unified set of institutions (if indeed they ever were). Media technologies have become a lot more accessible and user-friendly than they used to be – here it is only necessary to think of the examples of now routine mobile phones and social networking – and it is worth thinking about what this means for the *collective* aspect of panic.

How can invisible risks be known?

Of all the flight attempts caused by Fukushima, at first glance the one from the east of Russia to Moscow seems the oddest. The distance from Fukushima to the most eastern part of Russia is significant, with Korea and China in the way. Furthermore the wind was expected to blow south to Tokyo, and not west to Russia. So why were the flights to Moscow fully booked? According to a British newspaper report it was due to two factors. First of all, and as a computer engineer from Vladivostock explained, 'It's an old Soviet fear of a nuclear attack.' Second, the flight was explained as due to Russian memories of Chernobyl (McCurry and Booth 2011). This was the nuclear power station that exploded in April 1986, leading to the world's worst nuclear accident. The evident link of Russian flight to memories of Chernobyl and fears of nuclear war reinforces the argument about the cultural context of panic. There was a specifically post-Soviet dimension to the flight from eastern Russia, just as, of course, Fukushima being in Japan tied in with memories of the bombings of Hiroshima and Nagasaki. Peter Carey has shown how Japanese *anime* culture for example often draws on memories of destruction and nuclear fears (Carey 2005). The 1954 Japanese film *Godzilla* deals with nuclear mutation unleashed by human hubris. All of these cultural ingredients also went into the mix of making the precipitating event a cause of panic.

Social science can add another level of explanation to the panic about Fukushima. In the year of Chernobyl, Ulrich Beck published in Germany the book that was to appear in English translation in 1992 under the title *Risk Society*. Beck provided a new way of thinking about events like Chernobyl and, indeed, Fukushima. What is Beck's argument?

According to him, we live in a situation in which the old modern project of making nature useful for humans has had to start taking into account the side effects of this very project. In other words, whereas modernity could once be lived under the banner of 'progress' or 'wealth creation', now the situation is one of *reflexive modernization*, in which the confidence has been replaced with an awareness of the risks produced by what went before and what is done now. It is impossible to feign ignorance of the consequences of, say, power stations, for the stability of global ecosystems and human health. Thanks to air and water pollution and greenhouse gases it is now known that the technologies upon which modern life depends have consequences beyond original plans. These consequences might well be invisible at the moment but they are likely to break out in the future and, quite possibly, be utterly beyond control. For example nothing can be done to recover the nuclear wasteland around the Chernobyl plant. The modern dream of electrification has rebounded and created devastation. Similarly, nothing can be done to control the number of birth defects still being caused by the radiation which escaped when the plant went wrong. The modern dream of a world fit for humans, according to Beck, has led to a world that is risky for humans.

As the rather dead translation of Beck's book puts the matter: 'Questions of the development and employment of technologies ... are being eclipsed by questions of the political and economic "management" of the risks of actually or potentially utilized technologies' (Beck 1992: 19). Consequently: '*Risk may be defined as a systematic way of dealing with hazards and insecurities induced and introduced by modernization itself*' (Beck 1992: 23). Furthermore: 'the risks of civilization today typically *escape perception* and are localized in the sphere of *physical and chemical formulas* (e.g. toxins in foodstuffs or the nuclear threat)' (Beck 1992: 23). The 'radioactive wind' allegedly bearing down on Tokyo from Fukushima fits this definition rather precisely, although Beck does get it a little wrong. The risk does not reside in the formula. It resides in the actual toxins or radiation. Formulas of themselves are no more threatening than the words you are reading now.

For Beck, the ability of 'the risks of civilization today' to 'escape perception' – their *imperceptibility* – is exceptionally important. He uses this point to clarify the difference between modern industrial society and contemporary risk society. Beck gives the example of visitors to London and Paris in the nineteenth century and earlier. Both cities stank because of inadequate sewage disposal. The senses were assaulted, and the dangers to health were very immediately perceptible (Beck 1992: 21). This point can also be appreciated thanks to the novelist J.G. Ballard's memoir of growing up in Shanghai in the 1930s and 1940s: 'Open sewers fed into the stinking Whangpoo river, and the whole city reeked of dirt, disease and a miasma of cooking fat from the thousands of Chinese food vendors' (Ballard 2008: 6). Lest it be thought these attacks on perception were because Shanghai was then what might now be called a developing city, Ballard points out it was a trading city which was thoroughly and deeply connected with the wider world. Ballard's Shanghai was woven into the networks of interdependency. What Ballard encountered in Shanghai was exactly the situation that had also prevailed in London and Paris: 'In the past, the hazards could be traced back to an *under*supply of hygiene technology. Today they have their basis in industrial *over*production' (Beck 1992: 21). To put the matter directly: excrement is an intrinsic human problem, but nuclear radiation is not. Beck's imperceptible and invisible risks, 'are a *wholesale product* of industrialization, and are systematically intensified as it becomes global' (Beck 1992: 21). Indeed, the hazards in Shanghai today are due to industrialization rather than human bodies (although sewage disposal remains a problem). On 13 November 2010 monitors recorded a pollution index of 370 for the city. A score of 100 means 'polluted', and at 370 otherwise healthy people are likely to experience discomfort. The cause of the problem, evidently, was a change in the wind direction, so the wind was blowing the by-products of industrial plants over the city (Qian 2010). It was a side effect and to this extent typical of risk society. Furthermore, the awareness of the pollution and the need to do something to resolve the problem is distinctly *reflexive*.

Yet if the risks of risk society are not as obvious as sewage, if indeed they are as invisible as radiation, how can they be known? If it is impossible immediately to sense them, they must be knowable in some other way. What way? One answer to this question could be fairly straightforward. The risks of nuclear radiation for example might be beyond individual apprehension, but they are so obvious at a global level they simply cannot be ignored. Consequently they are reflexively known as problems. This is the nub of the point Anthony Giddens makes when he put forward what he rather immodestly entitled the 'Giddens paradox' in his discussion of climate change. It says: 'since the dangers posed by global warming aren't tangible, immediate or visible in the course of day-to-day life ... many will sit on their hands and do nothing of a concrete nature about them'. He concludes: 'Yet waiting until they become visible and acute before being stirred to serious action will, by definition, be too late' (Giddens 2009: 2). Put another way, it is immediately obvious when the sewers overflow, but radiation poisoning only approaches being unavoidable when people start becoming ill and, indeed, when the illnesses cannot be put down to some other possible causal factor. In this situation of the 'Giddens paradox' nuclear pollution, as with a risk like climate change, cannot be a cause of panic. If action takes place when it is too late (when people are already sick or the climate has already obviously changed), it is also action that will never be able to find a way out of the catastrophe. In other words it is action that might well be inspired by terror, but it cannot be inspired by panic. The 'Giddens paradox' essentially says don't panic because it's too late, and there is no longer an escape route. To pretend otherwise about the 'paradox' is nothing more than a victory of wishful thinking.

Second, science might have made the risk knowable through the generation of clear and unambiguous data. For instance the British government's 2006 review of the evidence on climate change by Lord Stern left little room for doubt as to the occurrence of global warming and its likely impact. The Stern Review was based on the scientific evidence and it is a classic document of the contemporary global risk society. It shows how 'greenhouse gases' are a by-product of industrialization causing global average temperatures to rise. Even though the heating up is imperceptible, and frequently goes hand in hand with local weather events which seem to contradict it, according to the Stern Review the evidence is stark and the implications of doing nothing are grave (Stern 2006). Yet in risk society scientific knowledge of the sort provided by Stern is not necessarily accepted. As Beck would immediately point out, the Stern Review looked at climate change from the point of view of its economic consequences alone. As such the Stern Review is organized around two different *rationalities of knowledge*. The review might be compelling, yet its full force is only felt if there is agreement about the economic consequences of climate change being the primary concern. A review that had concentrated on the biological implications of climate change would likely have been rather different, as would another approaching the issue exclusively from the point of view of water supplies. The Stern Review is scientifically objective yet it is also 'reliant on social and thus prescribed [from the point of view of science] expectations and values' (Beck 1992: 29). In other words for Stern's science to be entirely compelling there has to be agreement about the primacy of economic considerations, yet this agreement comes from the social and not the scientific sphere. However, scientific and social commitments are not necessarily compatible, and more likely they are in tension. This illustrates a point that Beck makes: 'what becomes clear in risk discussion are the fissures and gaps between scientific and social rationality in dealing with the hazardous potential of civilization. The two sides talk past each other' (Beck 1992: 30).

By this argument then, imperceptible and invisible risks are not known because they are revealed in all their horror by the objective truth of science. This is because lurking within the scientific project are social values which undermine from within any claims to universally legitimate scientific objectivity. The situation cannot be any different. As Beck puts it with a firm nod towards a maxim of Kant: 'scientific rationality without social rationality remains *empty*, but social rationality without scientific rationality remains *blind*' (Beck 1992: 30). For a perfect illustration of this claim it is only necessary to look at the very first sentence of the Executive Summary of the Stern Review: 'The scientific evidence is now overwhelming', it says: 'climate change presents very serious global risks, and it demands an urgent global response' (Stern 2006: i). The use of the word 'urgent' cannot be justified scientifically. Its justification can only come from social values. But without the use of the word, the findings of the Stern Review would be empty. They might well be scientifically valid and incontrovertible, but of themselves they would just be empty statements of facts. In the end then, whether or not there is acceptance of the findings of the Stern Review, or indeed of any other report on risks which escape perception, is only *partially* to do with science and the data it provides. Another explanation is needed, something to add to the *partial* explanation.

Third, most obviously and almost certainly most powerfully, the risks are known because they are covered by the media. Beck indeed emphasizes the media in his theory of risk society. The media are the sphere in which scientific rationality is filled with social relevance and in which social rationality is taken beyond its blindness. Beck defines the media as an agent, 'in charge of defining risks' (Beck 1992: 23). Consequently: 'The risk society is in this sense also the *science, media and information* society' (Beck 1992: 46). Specifically, the media are involved in, 'the demystification of scientific rationality in risk society' (Beck 1992: 197). This claim follows on from an assertion about how scientific reports and findings only become socially significant when they have been publicized in the media. These reports then become politically important because, according to Beck, once the media have established a risk problem it can only be ignored by the political class 'at the risk of losing votes' (Beck 1992: 197). As such the media do not just report risks, they actually *define* them too.

But how do some risks become so defined? It would seem to have little to do with the intrinsic quality of the scientific findings because, after all, of themselves they are empty. Something else makes the invisible and imperceptible risk socially relevant, and this happens through how: 'From the wealth of hypothetical findings, publication in the mass media selects specific examples which thereby achieve the addition of familiarity and credibility that they can no longer attain as pure scientific results' (Beck 1992: 197). Actually this is an extremely unhelpful comment by Beck because it is based on completely unexplained claims. Specifically, upon what basis do the media 'select specific examples' for publication? Beck's comments about media selection are very unclear. He says selection is not carried out on the basis of the 'power of editors' but instead on the ground of 'the editorial work of employees' who have an eye on audience figures (Beck 1992: 197). Beck almost certainly stresses 'employees' with a regard to audience figures rather than 'editors' because he wants to emphasize the social and sociological dimensions of the media. He is certainly wanting to get away from any hint of individualism according to which the editor has complete and controlling power. This is an important point. But Beck does not take it any further, and his distinction between editors and the 'editorial work of employees' seems to be more a theoretical nicety than an analytical insight.

But if it is hoped to understand how invisible risks are made into causes of panic, much more needs to be said about the media than this.

Are the media fascinating?

Let me make a strong assertion: *the risks to the contemporary networks of interdependency can only be known through the media*. This is because the risks are invisible, and precisely because they are invisible the media are required to fill in the details of the risk. And this is done according to media interests, not scientific or social ones.

This assertion begs a question. What are media interests? Here is Beck talking about the media: 'They have the ability to fascinate their audience, and by doing so, they can widen their economic possibilities' (Beck in Wimmer and Quandt 2006: 341). Here then the media are to be understood in economic terms – they are capitalist institutions – and they can maximize 'economic possibilities' (a phrase that presumably can be put more directly as 'profit') by 'fascinating' their audiences. This point needs to be stressed because it is so often forgotten in the academic study of the media. Beck is making a fundamental but oft-neglected point when he mentions the media's concerns to 'widen their economic possibilities'. In contemporary networks of interdependency *the dominant media interest is profit*. The media are *not* philanthropists, they are *not* playful semioticians, they are *not* direct agents of state dominance. No, media institutions *are* motivated by a primary interest in the generation and reproduction of profit. In as much as they are philanthropic or semiotically rich or in thrall to the state, it is because this helps secure the reproduction of profit. Similarly, and to put the matter with the brutal honesty it needs: media professionals might well enjoy their work but they do not do it out of a sense of charity. In the contemporary networks of interdependency, media professionals are able to work in the media because they sell a product with market value for both themselves and their employer.

The 'fascination' about which Beck talks consists in, 'waking people up, moving them and opening up their perspectives, even across borders' (Beck 1992: 197). On the basis of this 'fascination' audiences become knowledgeable political actors who have power because of their ability to say 'no'. After all, 'reports on discoveries of toxins in refuse dumps, if catapulted overnight into the headlines, change the political agenda. The established public opinion that the forests are dying compels new priorities' (Beck 1992: 197–8). These priorities will likely involve a refusal to support business generating the toxins. It is possible to think of other examples to illustrate the point. For instance, if the media report the tendency of a bank to gives its employees massive bonuses, the audience can be engaged and, on the basis of the engagement, this *fascination*, refuse to deal with the bank in question. It's good for everyone except the bank because, 'by offering this type of fascination, the media exercise their power and their market interest' (Beck in Wimmer and Quandt 2006: 341).

Traces of Habermas's discussion of the public sphere run through Beck's comments. First, for Beck and Habermas alike, the media constitute and generate areas of common concern. These concerns are raised in the media and then taken up to form a public debate around them. The media generate the concern and are the place in which public debate is carried out. Second, participants in the debate are encountered through their statements not their status, and therefore the public is a space of the formal equality of all participants. In principle I have as much ability to say something about the remuneration of bankers as the Governor of the Bank of England. Third, this public sphere is inclusive. Anyone can participate in it (Habermas 1989: 36). But there is a difference between Habermas and Beck. Habermas would be very doubtful whether the media's pursuit of, as Beck puts it, 'their market interest' is necessarily compatible with the encouragement of a public invested with the ability to say 'no'. After all, saying 'no' can extend to the media themselves. Yet for Beck the media can 'wake people up' and, in so doing, generate public debate which will enhance the role and therefore the 'market interest' of the media. For Beck, the more we are woken up the more we will want to know, and we come to know things through the media which, with an eye to the market, will always be trying to secure the largest audience possible.

But how is all of this achieved? Through, as Beck says, 'fascination'. But what is 'fascination'? Beck presumably meant the word in the sense of something being able to hold the attention through its intrinsic interest. Such a definition of the word would fit his overall argument rather well. However the word 'fascination' has another meaning, not necessarily incompatible with the first and yet pointing in a different direction. Fascination can also mean being entranced, captivated, put under a kind of spell. This is not a snide semantic point. The use of the word 'fascination' opens up the question of whether the media pursue their 'market interests' through a *captivation* of the audience, rather than the intrinsic interest of the story. It is certainly the implication of an argument developed by the media academic Susan Moeller.

Moeller talks about *compassion fatigue*, and if she is right the chances of media audiences being 'fascinated' in the first sense of the word (engaged by the intrinsic interest of the story) are increasingly slim if not, indeed, close to zero. This is because the media have already covered virtually every imaginable event, printed or broadcast the most harrowing images and exhausted some words of their meaning through overuse. According to Moeller this results in audience boredom and a lack of attention. A weary sense of 'we've seen it all before' or 'not this again' comes to dominate even responses to the most terrible stories of human suffering. This is the nub of compassion fatigue (Moeller 1999). Yet, as Moeller points out, the media still report these events. Although she does not make the point explicitly, the media carry on despite compassion fatigue because of – to use Beck's phrase again – 'market interest'. So, in the face of the boredom of audiences, how do the media secure their 'market interest'? Moeller's answer points towards the second meaning of the word 'fascination'. It points towards *attempts at deliberate captivation*.

Moeller looked at press coverage of human catastrophes, and identified three media responses to the compassion fatigue of their audiences. First, there emerges a dependency on tried and trusted formulas: 'If images of starving babies worked in the past to capture attention … then starving babies will headline the next difficult crisis' (Moeller 1999: 2). Second, there is always a concern to find the event or story that has never happened before. Everything has to be more deadly or dangerous than anything that has happened before. Here it is worth thinking about how the media consistently compared Fukushima to Chernobyl, and tried to establish which was worse. The point of the comparison was to try to make Fukushima worse because if it were not, then what was the big deal? As Moeller says, 'through a choice of language and images, the newest event is represented as being more extreme or deadly or risky than a similar past situation' (Moeller 1999: 2)[3.] Third, she says journalists are always worried they will be telling stories that are no longer interesting and this, 'encourages the media to move on to other stories once the range of possibilities of coverage have been exhausted so that boredom doesn't set in' (Moeller 1999: 2).

These points are significant because they show how the media's 'market interest' quite possibly leads to a style of reporting that is completely incompatible with the creation of a politically engaged and active public. For an example of this in the context of Fukushima it is worth looking at an astonishing article which appeared in the British tabloid *The Sun*. The paper is not terribly famous for its adherence to truth and has been known to spin stories in the past. But even by its own standards a front-page headline article about what it was like to live in post-Fukushima Tokyo was quite extraordinary.

Published on 17 March 2011, the piece was evidently based on a phone conversation between a *Sun* journalist and a woman who was introduced as British-born Keely Fujiyama, a resident of Tokyo with her Japanese husband and their two children. According to the journalist, Fujiyama described a Tokyo that had become an 'eerie ghost town' after the tsunami and radiation leak. Streets were said to be deserted, and water and fuel levels were getting worryingly low. Indeed, Fujiyama and her children were beginning to stare in the face of starvation. Their situation was dire: 'I'm scared, and shaky with hunger and really, really tired. I've got two hungry children and just a few crisps, oranges and a can of tuna', she said. 'I've had some juice today but I'm saving the rest for the children. There is no petrol, no water, no food.' Fujiyama plaintively cried: 'My children are already starving.' Their situation was so bad because they were taking official advice to stay indoors, and life was only sustainable because Fujiyama's husband was able to go shopping every evening on his return from work (I am very aware of what I have just written). However Keely Fujiyama had noticed how a car dealership was doing a roaring trade selling four-wheel drive vehicles to people desperate to flee from the city and into the country. She had been at the dealership with her husband a few days earlier despite the terrible petrol shortages (and again I know what I've just written. The story of Keely Fujiyama is told in Wheeler 2011).

To some degree it is a little unfair to pick on a newspaper article as stupid as this one about Keely Fujiyama (although it has done the career of the journalist, Virginia Wheeler, no harm. Despite the idiocy of the Keely Fujiyama story Wheeler stayed at *The Sun*, moving on to cover defence stories). But the story actually serves as a perfect illustration of Moeller's argument about how journalists try to deal with compassion fatigue. Had it been about a British woman managing to cope very well the story would have been boring and, indeed, it is unlikely it would have been published. There is no news value to a story about everything being fine. So the kinds of tricks identified by Moeller were used. First of all we have the heroic British woman stranded in a foreign land. Second her plight is unimaginable and like something from a blockbuster disaster film. Third, Keely Fujiyama quickly disappeared even before her story could become boring. Her tragic plight was never covered again, and the readers of *The Sun* would never know what happened next to this British woman and mother, starving until her husband brings home the shopping, watching people buy four-wheel drive vehicles to drive out of a city that was dry of petrol. If the readers remembered her in the first place of course. There was absolutely no response to the story in the pages of *The Sun* (although thanks to the Internet the story was picked up by other news agencies), and there is every indication it was completely forgotten. The paper's headline story the next day was 'War on Gaddafi', with side-bar items about the alleged sexual activity of a minor celebrity on a sun bed and, underneath, a few words on 'Race to airport by Brits'. The Tokyo panic was less important than celebrity gossip. The Keely Fujiyama story also shows how the 'market interest' of the media can too easily involve fascination through captivating stories rather than stories with an intrinsic interest in relation to risk. If invisible risks are communicated by the media, and if they carry stories like the one about Keely Fujiyama, there is no reason to share Beck's confidence in them.

There is another cause for concern about the impact of the media. Beck seems implicitly to assume a fairly straightforward model of the media. For him the media are a place of politics, but they exist independently of any given political practice and, indeed, as institutions that are distinct from the publics which form around them in the guise of readers, viewers or interlocutors. But this is now a very partial view of the media, one that has to be juxtaposed with a consideration of the impact of underinstitutionalized social media. Social media are having a massive impact on the knowledge of invisible risks and, furthermore, on panic in the circumstances of risk society.

At their best social media can be seen as a means of revitalizing the public sphere. This is because their cheapness and extraordinarily widespread availability makes it possible for people to come together to share views without having to pay any regard to status. Anyone can use social media, and therefore anyone is able to contribute their perspective to a concern shared by everyone. One journalist described a febrile atmosphere in Tokyo in which rumours,

> have spread like wildfire via mobile phones, infecting the city's 12 million people like a virus. Each new rumour sets phones buzzing in coffee shops and sushi restaurants, where customers are now fully conversant in the workings of nuclear reactors.

(Allen 2011)

But this is where the devil of social media resides too. First, if everyone can say their piece, expertise (of the kind necessary to solve a problem like Fukushima) becomes devalued. Second, the public status of concern changes. For Beck, the the public is consolidated in the communal act of saying 'no', but with social media the public instead becomes the external verification of the concerns of the individual – 'if other people think the same as me, I can't be wrong'. Third, precisely because social media make it possible for everyone to speak with an equal credibility (which is based entirely on the personal experience of the moment, and not necessarily, if at all, on any specialist knowledge), panic is exacerbated.

All of this happened in the days after Fukushima exploded and went into meltdown. Two themes run through the comments of many of the people interviewed by the media. First of all there was a collapse of trust in experts (but not in expert systems, as the willingness to use trains and planes shows). The experts were widely considered to be hiding something and, specifically, they were held to be trying to hide the truths which were known by the people who were trying to escape the radiation. After all, the argument seemed to run, people would not be fleeing without good reason, and therefore those who deny good reason must be operating to their own murky and self-seeking agendas. As one woman told a British journalist: 'The government is hiding what's really happened.' The justification for this statement seemed to come from the woman's friends, who like her were also attempting to leave Tokyo (Allen 2011). Expertise is democratized, but actually in a way that is profoundly unhelpful in the face of the kinds of risks emphasized by Beck. Andrew Gilligan spoke to a man who said:

> People are fed up with being told what to do and treated like fools. The problem with radiation is that you cannot know anything – you depend on the government for

the information to save your life. Now we are acting for ourselves, but the worry is that we left it too late.

(Gilligan 2011)

It's worth thinking about this comment a little because it points to the second theme that ran through a lot of the comments of people fleeing the radiation risk. They did not trust experts – they were happier instead to trust themselves or their friends – but they *also* wanted definite information from the very institutions that were otherwise condemned for treating people 'like fools'. Second, then, and in a mirror reflection of the first theme, the lack of trust in experts created a sense of insecurity – there was no one who could say what to do, there was no accepted and institutionally validated definition of the situation. The only trustworthy definitions were from people evidently having the same experiences as everyone else and communicating those experiences through social media. Consequently, the collective confirms the personal and justifies panic.

On the basis of this discussion it is possible to make a proposition:

> *In risk society, where invisible risks are necessarily mediated, panic is transformed. Panic happens, but not as a collective behaviour. Rather panic becomes the security of a collective validation of individualized confrontations with the fragility of networks of interdependency.* More precisely: *panic becomes a kind of safety in numbers; it is curiously reassuring.*

Conclusion

Panic reveals the fragility of the networks of interdependency. They are fragile because of the extent to which risk is implicit within them, both in terms of technological systems and the complexity of their spread, ultimately across the globe. Yet there is something historically novel about the connection of panic to technological risk. The risks are beyond apprehension and therefore beyond the place where they immediately happen (such as the prefecture of Fukushima). They have to be *communicated* and are only known through the media. All of these points are valid. However it is necessary to think a little more about the media and to think about them not just as technologies of communication but also in terms of their impact on the knowledge of audiences.

Obviously the development of social media muddies the situation completely. On the one hand they offer the possibility of the communication of experiences and voices that might well run directly contrary to the institutionalized media. Social media certainly imply the communication of a more diverse and subtle range of stories than national television broadcasters, for instance, can facilitate. Yet on the other hand, the very democracy of social media leads to a situation in which each voice becomes equal with any other. This is the basis of some confused claims about the possibilities they imply. Once social media are seen in this way, as a technology making one voice equal with any other, it is possible to see them as a necessarily politically democratic technology. But they are not, or at least not *necessarily*. First of all, in some situations some voices do need to count for more than others. Here it is only necessary to think about Fukushima. The average citizen would have no idea whatsoever about how to go about solving the problems at the crippled plant. Second, the multiplication of equal voices undermines the possibility of any coherent definition of the situation. For example, Keely Fujiyama's voice has the same status as everyone and anyone else's even though what she had to say – assuming she actually said it – was stupid. The very democracy of social media can create confusion. Rowan Williams once made an excellent point. He was thinking of the dominant institutionalized media, but the point applies even more strongly when it is read in the context of social media: 'so far from guaranteeing that we are aware of what is currently going on in the world, we end up with no clear apprehension at all of a real present moment' (Williams 2000: 89).

The 'real present moment' dissolves in a kaleidoscope of juxtapositions. First, any given moment dissolves into the wider context of different personal encounters. *This* happened to *me* and *this* happened to *me* and *this* happened to *me*. Second, time fractures especially in as much as media (either institutionalized or social) are globalized. For example, the 9/11 attacks on the World Trade Center were timed to hit New York at the beginning of the working day, but in Europe they happened in the early to mid-afternoon. So when did they happen? Third, because social media multiply voices and indeed coexist with institutionalized media, each is engaged in a struggle to secure an increasingly fractured audience. Consequently the audience is encouraged to *choose* precisely what the moment will contain. Will time be spent with these media or with another? And does each medium deal with the same events and indeed attribute to them the same meaning? Do they all associate the 'real present moment' with the same contents? There is no reason to assume the answer is 'yes'. There is no single definition of the 'real present moment'. Different media will define it differently and perhaps even give it varying content in terms of attempts to secure an audience. As such the very sense of a real present moment becomes dependent upon techniques of persuasion. The media are not, then, the neutral reporters of Beck's imagining.

Media also complicate the meaning of social space. Such a complication is also implied by the networks of interdependency that make 'here' dependent on 'there' (the air in Tokyo dependent on the air in Fukushima, for instance). But the media take the situation further. The 'here' is made to be nowhere special through its juxtaposition with lots of 'theres'. Nevertheless, the 'here' is the pivot around which the world turns for the individual. But this has serious interpretative implications. Quite simply, the 'here' is the *locus* in which acts of interpretation are required to occur. But what the media – social or institutionalized – put into the *locus* is beyond its independent ability to make sensible. This has three consequences. First, because independent resources are swamped, there is dependency on others to explain what is happening. There is a collapse of confidence in independent interpretative competence. Then again experts aren't necessarily trusted either because every voice counts the same. Second, the *locus* seems to become the target of a risky world and therefore it has to be protected from the outside. Third, as part of the defence the *locus* needs an ability to shut out the world, and one of the best ways of doing this is, precisely, through the consumption of the products of other media, especially entertainment. This is because they offer in 'here' compensations for, or distractions from, what happens out 'there'.

The upshot of all this *is the subordination of knowledge to information*. The distinction is taken from Walter Benjamin who said:

> Every morning brings us the news of the globe, and yet we are poor in noteworthy stories. This is because no event any longer comes to us without already being shot through with explanation. In other words, by now almost nothing that happens benefits storytelling: almost everything benefits information.
>
> *(Benjamin 1973: 89)*

According to Benjamin, storytelling leads to knowledge because it transforms the event into something making sense. Knowledge exists when the event can be reconciled with experience through the story. But the multiplication of media, and of course Benjamin was writing long before social media were even a glimmer, dissolves the present moment. As such knowledge becomes validated by quantity not quality. The experts come to represent a small and specialized voice which cannot count for any more than the loud shouting of all the people who know what is really going on because they have managed to access Facebook via their cell phones.

2
PANIC AND MORALITY

There is something a little odd about Beck's risk society thesis. It's worth thinking about how it works as a mode of rhetoric. On the one hand, and in order to confirm the validity of his thesis, Beck is required to emphasize the risks associated with nuclear technology and so on. If he did not do this there would be nothing to say, no reason to engage with his theory. However, on the other hand, he is required to hold out the possibility of a response to the risks so as to avoid any accusation of despair. He talks about how politics ought and still could, 'lay down the overall (juridical) conditions, check the general applicability of regulations and produce consensus' (Beck 1992: 235). Or, put another way, politics can overcome risk. So is the panic of risk society actually technological or political? Furthermore, this presumes a politics based on reason and the acceptance of expert knowledge. There is unfortunately no reason to presume this kind of politics in contemporary circumstances where traditional media institutions and technologies are now having to grapple with the impact of social media.

Obviously it would be ridiculous to dismiss the risks of nuclear and other technologies. But maybe if we want to get some kind of grip on the *panic* they imply it is necessary to go back to an earlier stage of nuclear history. For us nuclear technology simply 'is'. It has become an intrinsic aspect of the contemporary world, and so for us the problem is really an administrative one. Nuclear technology is not going to go away. It cannot be 'disinvented'. The situation has not always been like this. Once nuclear technology was *not* commonplace. Once the nuclear was *challenging*. It is worth returning to the *moment* of challenge, to the moment of confrontation with nuclear technology. This might help with the work of recovering some sense of the enormity of the technology, some of the sense that has been lost. It is noticeable how, despite everything, Beck is confident he knows the answers to the nuclear question, but at the dawn of the nuclear era, after the bombing of Hiroshima and Nagasaki, people were staring into an abyss. They now had to deal with a question for which there was no ready answer and indeed no existing framework of understanding. Everything that might have been previously taken for granted had been challenged by the events that ended the Second World War, and this was even before the revelation of the full horror of the Nazi Holocaust. In the first attempts to come to terms with the nuclear challenge it is possible to see intimations of the widest extent and depths of modern panic.

> *Modern panic is not just about risk. Rather the awareness of risk is a dim recollection of the metaphysical panic which was caused by the dawn of the nuclear age.*

The lack of answers to the nuclear panic was expressed at the beginning of a thorough and fascinating report published by the British Council of Churches in May 1946, well within a year of the August 1945 bombings. The prose is measured, but even so the enormity of the nuclear challenge gets through: 'It would be the extremity of short-sightedness to proceed complacently with preconceived plans and normal activities, as though nothing revolutionary had happened, more particularly since misuse of the new energy might at a stroke reduce such activities to insignificance' (British Council of Churches 1946: 7). Such activities would of course be made insignificant because now we might all be simultaneously incinerated. Indeed, the report identified this as the central question raised by the nuclear age. This was because thanks to Hiroshima and Nagasaki it was no longer possible to take the future for granted. Consequently, no one could be presumed to be wanting to do anything that would only flourish in the future. Since there can be no confidence in there actually being a future, there is no longer any point doing anything that stretches beyond the here and now. According to the report, men and women only 'leave the fruits of their work to be gathered in large part by their descendants ... because they have felt that their work will be allowed to endure' (British Council of Churches 1946: 16). The lesson of Hiroshima and Nagasaki pointed in exactly the opposite direction. Maybe nothing can endure an atomic explosion. Confidence in the future was burnt along with buildings and victims.

This was immensely important, because according to the British Council of Churches report: 'The loss of that confidence will inevitably destroy the fundamental conditions for many of the best qualities in our present civilisation' (1946: 16). 'Already' the report announced, and remember this was less than a year after the nuclear bombs were dropped,

> we can observe a sense of the futility of much that has seemed most worth while in the past ... Western civilisation has now little else to put in the place of the hope which inspired men in the past. When hope gives way to despair ... the only alternative left open is recklessness. This does at least seem to fill the void which has been created.
>
> *(British Council of Churches 1946: 17)*

This sense was to be captured extraordinarily well by Colin Self, perhaps the most interesting British pop artist of the 1960s. His 1962–63 painting *Waiting Women and Two Nuclear Weapons (Handley Page Victors)* shows a group of women dressed up for a fashionable party (although one wears a swimming costume) as two bombers fly overhead, unnoticed and ignored.[1] The title of the painting therefore raises the question: for what kind of oblivion are these women waiting? Alcoholic or atomic? Or both?

At its grandest then, the panic borne of the nuclear age is one about human *immortality*. As the British Council of Churches report said it is necessary to confront, 'the feelings of insecurity, anxiety and futility engendered in many minds by the prospect of the sudden extinction of civilised life. Men can hardly be expected to spend their strength and to sacrifice themselves for far-off ends ... if their confidence in the future has been gravely undermined'. In fact for the authors of the report, 'There is no more powerful solvent of society ... than the belief that life is essentially impermanent and that we are in the grip of forces which we are without power to control' (British Council of Churches 1946: 19). Social life needs a metaphysical depth if it is going to reconcile men and women to their own transience. It needs something to underpin confidence in the permanent and enduring. We can only deal with our own mortality if it is reinforced by trust in the immortal.

Hiroshima and Nagasaki destroyed the accepted dreams of immortality. There is absolutely no reason to be confident about the endurance of our achievements for even a millisecond after our death. Never before have men and women had the dreadful knowledge we share. The moment of the death of one woman could be the moment of the death of all women. What follows? As soon as this question is raised the discussion inexorably points to Dostoevsky. Although the specifically nuclear panic might be new, the seeds of metaphysical panic were planted in the nineteenth century and explored in the great novels. But there is a difference.

Dostoevsky's characters played games with their metaphysical panic, whereas we live with it as an intrinsic part of the human condition (except when we can forget it by going to parties instead).

For these purposes, Dostoevsky's most valuable novel is *The Brothers Karamazov*. Dostoevsky attributed to one of the three brothers, Ivan Karamazov, a very stark view of the human condition: 'were mankind's belief in its immortality to be destroyed, not only love but also any living power to continue the life of the world would at once dry up in it. Not only that, but then nothing would be immoral any longer' (Dostoevsky 1992: 69). Note how Ivan Karamazov's argument was evidently offered in the spirit of a *conjecture* (he explores what would happen *if* the belief in immortality *were* to be destroyed), whereas we know the belief has been pushed to the margins by events. In secular terms it is no longer possible to use a word like 'immortality' without it being received in a spirit of irony. According to the view attributed to Ivan Karamazov then, where there is *mortality* there is *immorality* because there is nothing to give 'living power' to morality. The character of Ivan Karamazov evidently took this insight to a logical conclusion:

> for every separate person, like ourselves for instance, who believes neither in God nor his own immortality … egoism, even to the point of evildoing, should not only be permitted … but should be acknowledged as the necessary, the most reasonable, and all but the noblest result of his situation.
>
> *(Dostoevsky 1992: 69)*

Another character in the novel summarized this view: 'If there is no immortality of the soul, then there is no virtue, and therefore everything is permitted' (Dostoevsky 1992: 82).

This is the essence of *metaphysical panic*. It dissolves morality and puts the egoistic individual at the centre of the social stage. The door of immortality has slammed shut, but the draught has opened other doors. The picture turns back to Colin Self's painting of happily smiling women waiting for oblivion of one sort or another. However, if this metaphysical panic infiltrates into social life the networks of interdependency collapse. First of all, and as the British Council of Churches report showed, if there is no confidence in a future there is unlikely to be any great commitment to the establishment of institutions or practices which are intended to endure. Instead there will be 'recklessness'. The authors of the report probably had an eye to personal behaviour when they spoke about recklessness, but arguably it has also become the defining characteristic of global financial markets. They are evidently engaged in a reckless pursuit of profit *now*, without regard to any future stretching beyond the next computerized transaction. A similar focus on the short term runs through the energy industry. Hans-Werner Sinn has shown how fossil fuel extraction is about short-term profit. On the one hand many of the oil-producing states are unstable and therefore want to get as much money as they can before their downfall, and on the other hand presently the costs of extraction do not have to compensate for environmental damage, and so profit-seeking companies seek to extract as much as they can before they might have to take such costs into consideration (Sinn 2012). Second, recklessness also implies the kind of egoism about which Dostoevsky's Ivan Karamazov evidently spoke. If there is no future there is no immortality, and consequently there is absolutely no reason not to follow one's own desires – regardless of what they might be and entail – in the here and now. After all there are no firm moral rules to stop me, no eternity in which I will pay the price. I'm here today, gone tomorrow, so why not just do what I want in the meantime? And on what possible basis might you condemn me?

Metaphysical panic is real and terrible. But let's be honest, most people do not confront metaphysical panic most of the time. Most of us are more like Colin Self's waiting women.

The networks of interdependency might well be fragile, but they have not collapsed. For proof of this claim, it is necessary only to think about the complex networks that have taken these sentences from my computer to you. Furthermore, we might well have trouble saying what is moral, but we find it pretty easy to condemn some people and some actions as immoral. Even if egoism is accepted (and indeed nurtured by consumerism), nevertheless we are ready and content to condemn when some people become *too* egoistic and forget about others. Put another way, there are very effective designs for living in the shadow of metaphysical panic.

What are these designs? How is it possible to carry on when metaphysical panic is real? These are the questions I want to explore in this chapter. But I want to explore them in a way that might seem a little startling at first. I want us always to bear Colin Self's waiting women in mind, and I want us to think about why they are so happy even as the bombers fly behind them. I think there are very mundane answers to these rather big questions. They are happy because despite everything the world makes sense, they are happy because they know who to blame when things go wrong, they are happy because they are able to panic about other things than nuclear apocalypse and metaphysical emptiness. This takes me to the claim that might be considered a little startling, and maybe it is but I am deadly serious. Like Colin Self's women we are able to put aside metaphysical panic because we are situated in a world saturated by — and now indivisible from, impossible and inconceivable without — the media. The media have transcended metaphysics, and they have done this because they, first, assert a morality that is validated by its negation not its affirmation and, second, because this validation naturalizes the networks of interdependency by pointing to groups that are a threat and allegedly in need of discipline. This is the full importance of the social science and media studies literature on *moral panics* — a full significance that has been missed because the concept of moral panics was too quickly pulled within disciplinary boundaries and turned into a tool for almost machine-produced analysis rather than what it might have been, a lever on the world (see also McRobbie and Thornton 1995: 561).

This chapter has two main sections. In the first section I will discuss the key existing literature on moral panics. In this section it will be shown how moral panics emphasize the role of the media in providing ways of understanding a changing of the world. In this way the media are doing rather more than being moral entrepreneurs or the agents of state hegemony. In the second section I will take up the other strand of the moral panic debate: folk devils. The existing literature tends to take 'snapshots' of folk devils and little attempt is made to draw out what they all share in common beyond their erstwhile deviance (and of course the category of 'deviance' implicitly normalizes the routine and institutionally sanctioned). So, in this section it will be shown how folk devils are groups that are presented and understood to be *outsiders* in relation to the *established* routine practices required by the existing networks of interdependency. I guess my main concern in this chapter is to try to release the idea of moral panics from the disciplinary straitjackets in which it was too quickly, and is now too easily, imprisoned.

What is a moral panic?

It would be fascinating to know for sure what the British Council of Churches report had in mind when it spoke about 'recklessness'. Fairly informed guesses can be made though. The report is worried about sexual relationships and in particular contraception. Writing the problem on the metaphysical terrain the report wonders if people will carry on having children if they have no hope in the future, if they have no faith in the endurance of the human world. But the concern is immediately brought down to earth because this is identified as the first time in history when 'the failure of faith in the continuity of society would be accompanied by the power to limit the number of children brought into the world'. This concern then moved on to one about stable relationships. The atomic world implies, 'a state of insecurity [in which] most men and women would be forced back into a life that accepted impermanence as something inevitable, and would live only for the present' (British Council of Churches 1946: 17).

The report was not the only place where this kind of view was expressed. In his panoramic history of post-war Britain, David Kynaston quotes David Mace of the Marriage Guidance Council. In September 1945, a month after the bombs had dropped, Mace said: 'There is no sense of stability ... We are forced to live in the "here and now" because we just do not know about tomorrow ... The atomic bomb "question mark" means that it is no good planning' (Kynaston 2007: 109). Evidence of the lack of stability seemed to be all around and multiplying. There were 12,314 divorces in England and Wales in 1944, and 60,190 in 1947 (Kynaston 2007: 97). Sexual morality was becoming complicated. Earlier conventions about sex outside marriage were collapsing, although extra-marital affairs were largely condemned. Kynaston uses Mass Observation data to paint a picture of increasing anxiety about what was happening and what could be considered to be permissible (Kynaston 2007: 375). People already seem as if they are thinking about going to the party with Colin Self's waiting women. This is actually an early glimpse of a moral panic, and like all such panics it reflects then contemporary concerns about the fragility of the networks of interdependency. The focus was on the interdependency of the family relationships which were being put under strain by the return of men from the war, to women who had become independent in the labour market. Indeed what makes it a *moral* panic as opposed to simply a panic is the connection of fragility to the actions of men and women. Whereas risk is about systemic panic, when panic becomes moral it is about how the actions of certain groups are taken to imply fragility. Moral panic is focused on the disorderly social event.

An anticipation of what was to come to be called a moral panic can also be found in a study from the United States. Fred Fejes has explored a panic about child abduction in Miami. In July 1954 a 7-year-old girl was abducted, raped and murdered. The incident sparked a press campaign against 'perverts', and this in turn led to a focus on the local gay male community. The focus was tightened a few weeks later when a male airline steward was murdered by two young men he had met in a gay bar. In these few weeks the status of Miami's gay community was transformed: 'Previously homosexuals had been regarded as a colorful if somewhat embarrassing part of the Miami night-life and beach scene; now they were seen as a serious threat to the safety and moral wellbeing of the community' (Fejes 2000: 306).

The fascinating aspect of Fejes's study is how it connects this panic to the transformation of Miami itself. This was not just a panic about 'perverts' as it appeared superficially to be. As Fejes shows it was actually a panic about the fragility of Miami as it experienced rapid social change. Between 1945 and 1955 the population grew by 126 per cent. The place was changing from a beach resort to a modern city and drawing in new residents. This not only caused a range of infrastructural problems, it also had a social effect. As Fejes puts it, there was a profound sense of 'lack of deep rootedness'.

> Many came to the area because of climate, not because of economic opportunity. Many were only part-time residents, returning North for the summer. For those seeking to be full-time residents, it was often difficult to find jobs or start businesses and the turnover in population was fairly large.
>
> *(Fejes 2000: 309)*

The political structure had failed to change to cope with what was happening in the city, and therefore only the media could make any claim to represent the 'community'. Yet this media spoke for and to a Miami that was uncertain about its identity, and therefore it had to create a sense of what it meant to be the kind of person 'who lives here'. This happened through a panic which reflected the fragile interdependency of rapidly changing Miami and which established 'who we are' by pointing to others and saying 'we're not like them'. As Fejes says of the media campaign:

> the ultimate goal was not to drive the "perverts" out of town ... Rather, the goal was to guarantee that homosexuality be regarded as a stigmatized behavior for which, like gambling, petty corruption, and other acceptable pre-war vices, there would be no public tolerance.
> *(Fejes 2000: 342)*

The stories of Fejes and the British Council of Churches report dovetail nicely. The details might well be different, but both panics are similar. They are both trying to understand who 'we are' in the circumstances in which what could be previously taken for granted no longer applies in a rapidly changing situation. There is an attempt to shore up a building on shifting sand through what amounts to intolerance which is, however, presented as being *moral*. This is a hidden theme in the British Council of Churches report, and an explicit one in the media campaign studied by Fejes.

It is important to be clear about precisely what the word 'moral' means in this sense. It does not mean *universal* criteria of right and wrong, good and bad. After all if it did our examples would require a conclusion about the wrongness of, just to start, contraception, sexual relationships outside marriage, homosexuality and so forth. By reverse neither does the word morality require a conclusion about criteria of right and wrong, good and bad being entirely *social constructs*, reducible to the time and place in which they are expressed. If such were the case we would end up with some very difficult arguments. The banal observation here centres on the ancient Greek lack of concern about sexual relationships between young boys and older men. Neither is morality identical with *law*. Again, if it were some horrific conclusions are reached, the most obvious of which is simply to point out how the law in Nazi Germany encouraged discrimination against Jews.

So what then is the meaning of the word 'moral' which comes out of our examples? Well, it's a *sociological* definition in which the moral is defined by negation. The moral consists in the good and right which is practically confirmed – but not stated as such – by the self-evident bad and wrong perpetrated by groups who are 'not like us'. Their actions are bad and wrong because they intimate the fragility of networks of interdependency. In other words, from a sociological point of view morality is about definitions, and the definitions operate in such a way as to connect the moral with the routine, the institutional and the predictable. The moral is that which confirms networks of interdependency. From the perspective of the routine, institutionalized and predictable, anything that is not routine, institutionalized and predictable is defined as immoral and is likely the cause of a moral panic. This moral panic reconfirms the moral goodness of the existing order of things. The definitional activity can take place because institutions exercise power. They have the power to say 'no' without at any time having clearly to state what is good and right. Consequently, and by this definition, no small part of the panic in a moral panic comes from the refusal of certain groups to accept the 'no'. The threat they represent is nothing less than one of *deinstitutionalization*.

Now, if these points are all borne in mind, and if the emergence of the phrase 'moral panic' can be identified in a definite time and place – as it can, England in the 1960s – two points follow. First the phrase 'moral panic' must attend to transformations being experienced in the time and place (England in the 1960s). It must be historically specific. To this extent when Fejes reads the 1954 case as a moral panic, and when I identify traces of moral panic in the British Council of Churches report we can both be accused of using a distinctly contemporary concept and projecting it back into the past. This of course creates the methodological problem of it thereby being relatively easy to find what you are looking for (but for a discussion of some attempts to do just this, see Hunt 1997). Second, the moral panics ought to focus on 'deviant' groups, with the deviance being located in their denial of the institutionalized 'no', their unpredictability and in all the challenge they evidently represent to routine. They are able to represent such a challenge because they are outside of the networks of interdependency.

These themes do indeed come out in a reflection by Jock Young. He was one of the people to start the whole moral panic debate and he is very clear about the social situation in which he wrote. According to Young, the idea of moral panics emerged from, and spoke to,

> a time when the postwar disciplines of restraint and deferred gratification were breaking down; they were times of seeming progress yet of increased social instability: the movement into late modernity ... The moral panics coalesced around the feelings of *ressentiment* with regard to an older generation against youth cultures which carried with them harbingers of the future.
>
> *(Young 2011: 255–6)*

Here then is both social context and the recognition of the emphasis on certain groups. What Young says is reinforced by Stanley Cohen, with whom the phrase 'moral panic' is now inextricably associated thanks to his use of it in the title of his book, *Folk Devils and Moral Panics*, which was first published in 1972 (I am using the third edition of the book and shall therefore refer to Cohen 2002).

For Cohen, the social context that is the background of moral panics in Britain in the 1960s was marked by post-war affluence and, in particular, the emergence of youth as a group of consumers. As Cohen put it:

> There was a large unmarried teenage generation ... whose average real wage had increased at twice the rate of the adults'. The relative economic emancipation created a group with few social ties or responsibilities and whose stage of development could not really be managed by the nuclear working-class family.
>
> *(Cohen 2002: 203)*

In other words, social change had created a situation in which a new group had emerged which did not readily fit with the established networks of interdependency. They were teenagers and therefore young enough to live with their parents, and yet they had independent consumer power, and capitalist industries were quick to exploit this through the creation of generation-specific styles of dress, music and leisure. But, as Cohen points out, the teenagers of the late 1950s and early 1960s (presumably these are the children of the 'recklessness' that concerned the writers of the British Council of Churches report) were not simple victims of capitalism. They also used and manipulated consumer goods for their own purposes of distanciation and differentiation. Consequently, 'the emerging styles became associated with deviant or publicly disapproved values' (Cohen 2002: 203). All of this set the stage for a moral panic about teenagers in Britain and, as Cohen's study showed, this coalesced around the conflicts between gangs like the Mods and Rockers. Their fights in places like Brighton on bank holidays in the early to mid-1960s provided the precipitating social event for moral panic.[2]

So what then is a moral panic? The first paragraph of the first chapter of Cohen's book provides the classic definition:

> societies appear to be subject, every now and then, to periods of moral panic. A condition, episode, person or group of persons emerges to become defined as a threat to societal values and interests; its nature is presented in a stylized and stereotypical fashion by the mass media ... Sometimes the object of the panic is quite novel and at other times it is something which has been in existence long enough, but suddenly appears in the limelight. Sometimes the panic passes over and is forgotten, except in folklore and collective memory; at other times it has more serious and long-lasting repercussions.
>
> *(Cohen 2002: 1)*

A moral panic consequently occurs when a precipitating social event – an action carried out by a defined and definable type of person or group – is seen as a threat to 'societal values and interests'. Cohen's way of putting this point is significant since it shows how these values and interests are not known through their affirmation and declaration, so much as through the negation and sense of threat implied by the precipitating event. And of course Cohen's definition emphasizes the role of the media in the generation of moral panics. Indeed, without the media there would and could be no moral panic. Why?

Although Cohen does not make the point explicitly, the media are crucial in moral panics for two reasons. First of all, the precipitating social event is not directly experienced by most of the people who come to share in some sense of panic. However it is important to be methodologically cautious here. To make a claim about a moral panic in the media does not of itself justify a corollary claim about a moral panic amongst populations. This point can be too easily forgotten when moral panic studies are machine-produced. It would be worth thinking about why sometimes a moral panic in the media *fails* to translate into more widespread social panic. Second, the media establish the contours of the panic by making it readily identifiable with certain persons or groups. Put simply, the media tell us what to look for as the signs of peril to the values and interests we cannot really put into words but know when they are threatened. Cohen says: 'The media have long operated as agents of moral indignation in their own right ... their reporting of certain "facts" can be sufficient to generate concern, anxiety, indignation or panic' (Cohen 2002: 9–10).

All of this happens because of a distinctive cycle in the media creation of moral panics. First, there is an initial act (in Smelser's terms a precipitating event) which is taken to be threatening. This is defined by the media as worthy of attention and investigation and there is an encouragement of the condemnation of the actors. Second, all persons or groups that are linked through stereotypes to the act are isolated from wider social relationships, and in response those so stigmatized, 'perceive themselves as more deviant, group themselves with others in a similar position, and this leads to more deviance' (Cohen 2002: 11–12). There is an increase in deviance for two reasons: now the group has been identified everything it does is taken to be deviant more or less by definition and furthermore because the group takes on its stigmatization as a badge of identity and validation. This is precisely what happened in the United Kingdom with the introduction of Anti-Social Behaviour Orders in 1998. Third, since the actions and style of the group evidently justify the initial panic about them, the group is subjected to even more condemnation. This cycle of amplification goes round and round, although Cohen is subtle enough to appreciate there is nothing inevitable about the amplification cycle continuing indefinitely. The continuation of the cycle depends on such external considerations as news values, other precipitating events, the extent to which the media-amplified panic speaks to wider concerns about social values (Cohen 2002: 12).

Clearly Cohen's perspective on the media assumes they are the defenders of established values and therefore play a politically conservative role when they engage in moral panics. By Cohen's analysis the media work in terms of the identification and condemnation of threats, and thereby support the status quo. The media are moral entrepreneurs. They are rule creators who demand action on the part of rule enforcers to deal with the threat to order (Becker 1963). Cohen however points out the dilemma confronting these moral entrepreneurs. Drawing on the work of Howard Becker, Cohen notes how they can only defend the status quo by, first, saying the condemnation works and yet, second, by identifying a worsening of the situation (Cohen 2002: 52). After all, if the threat really was overcome the moral entrepreneurs would have done themselves out of a job. Perhaps this explains why moral panics often quickly disappear. Maybe they are removed before they are resolved. Yet these are relatively under-explored themes in Cohen's book and indeed his attempt to address the politics of the analysis of moral panics does not really add too much clarity to the debate (Cohen 2011).

The same cannot be said for the way the analysis of moral panics was taken up and used by Stuart Hall and his colleagues at the Birmingham Centre for Contemporary Cultural Studies. In their book *Policing the Crisis* they sought to show how the panic about mugging in 1970s Britain could be understood as a hegemonic strategy carried out by the ideological state apparatus of the media and the repressive state apparatus of the police and legal system to secure consent around new and intrusive practices of the imposition of 'law and order'. The focus of these practices was upon the alleged criminality of young African-Caribbean men. This group could be readily identified by ethnicity, stigmatized through its style of dress and indeed its alleged distinctive mode of criminality (operating in gangs to rob people on the street), and therefore condemned as a threat to moral order which needed to be heavily policed

(Hall *et al.* 1979). For Hall and his colleagues there was a political imperative to resist the moral panic over mugging. The extent to which the mugging study has become influential in the study of moral panics perhaps shows better than anything else how the potential of Cohen's approach has been closed down by disciplinary conventions. The Birmingham study works well in its own terms (although there is the typical Cultural Studies weakness of never using a simple word when a bit of theory can be dropped in instead), but as Waddington points out it actually lacks empirical validity. Put another way, what *Policing the Crisis* argues, and the conclusions it reaches about moral panic and the state, are simply invalid (Waddington 1986). This influential book is more interesting as a disciplinary phenomenon than as an analysis of moral panic. However this is emphatically not to deny that African-Caribbean men were subjected to a media campaign of vilification and policed in what can only be called a racist way.

Why are they folk devils?

Let's pull together the threads of the argument so far. The 'atomic age' brought about a condition of metaphysical panic. The doors were slamming on the future and on any human ambitions stretching beyond the here and now. Everything was seen to be entering a state of profound fragility and it was impossible to identify stabilizers. This sense is conveyed very powerfully in many of the films made by Ingmar Bergman in the 1950s and Michelangelo Antonioni in the early 1960s. Yet somehow we have been able to stop worrying about the bomb and actually achieve a morally meaningful social life. Colin Self painted one way in which this can happen when he offered his women going to the universal party-time.

However there is a more mundane way in which we have been able to stop worrying. Metaphysical panic has been swamped by the proliferation and insinuation of the media through social life and, indeed, imagination. This has happened through a kind of pincer movement. On the one fork the media are part of a voracious profit-seeking capitalism which creates new markets for itself, and on the other there has been nothing to stop their flooding of imagination. They filled the metaphysical vacuum with the things of this world alone. The media make the world make a kind of sense and, in the case of morality, this is done through negation without need for reference to troublesome concepts like value or virtue. Like Dostoevsky's characters we are unable to say in what the right and good consists, but we are easily able to identify those who are not right and good. Those who are so identified are the precipitators of moral panic. They cause panic because they highlight the fragility of the networks of interdependency through their evident refusal to accept the routine and predictability of institutionalized action.

Cohen famously called these precipitators of panic by the name *folk devils,* and he says they are, quite simply, 'visible reminders of what we should not be' (Cohen 2002: 2). This is a useful definition and even in so few words it implies a readily operable research programme. But one of the interesting things about Cohen's book is how it goes no further in providing a definition of the phrase 'folk devil'. The term is validated in its use. This oddity has arguably been disguised by the sheer deluge of papers identifying folk devils and showing how they are constructed by and in the media. In many ways then the strength of Cohen's book – its insight, its ability to suggest a research programme, its accessibility – has perhaps been the biggest problem to befall the debate about folk devils. Cohen showed us 'how to do it', and it has indeed been done with very few questions being asked about the exact status of the category of the folk devil. Consequently it is possible to construct a long list of folk devils, but what they have in common is merely circular. Folk devils are those whom the media represent as being reminders of 'what we should not be' and such reminders are folk devils. But arguably the social type of the folk devil is much more important than this, and considerably more capable of levering open an analysis of the sociology of panic.

> *Folk devils are not just media constructs. They are also the symbolization of the fragility of networks of interdependency. More precisely: folk devils cause panic because they are outsiders to the established networks of interdependency.*

The identification of folk devils as outsiders to established networks deliberately gestures towards work by the sociologist Norbert Elias. In the early 1960s he carried out a community study with John Scotson. They were interested in the disdain in which one group of residents in a town near Leicester held another group. This was despite the absence of all the usual sociological factors which might explain the disregard. The two groups were more or less identical in terms of class, income, housing and ethnicity. And yet one group thought itself to be 'better' than the other. What made the difference? The variable factor upon which Elias and Scotson focused was, quite simply, duration of residence and the ability following from this to possess control of local institutions, as well as to enjoy cohesive social relationships and shared attitudes made routine over time. Those who had become *established* in the town looked down upon those who had only recently arrived and who were identified (and who indeed identified themselves) as *outsiders*. After all they threw into relief everything the established took for granted but barely knew they had until they came to encounter its absence thanks to the presence of the outsiders. And so the outsiders became inferior and tainted, to be avoided wherever possible. As Elias put it in his sole-authored reflection on the study with Scotson: 'the established group attributed to its members superior human characteristics; it excluded all members of the other groups from non-occupational social contact with its own members'.

He went on: 'the taboo on such contacts was kept alive by means of social control such as praise-gossip about those who observed it and the threat of blame-gossip against suspected others' (Elias and Scotson 1994: xvi). The established made sure they had as little as possible to do with the outsiders, all the easier to be able to condemn them as not worth knowing.

For Elias this community study had done nothing other than reveal one of the most fundamental figurational relationships underpinning social life itself, regardless of time and place. It revealed how one group is able to distinguish itself from another and, indeed, to see the other as – to put it into Cohen's and not Elias's terms – a *folk devil*. The shift from Elias's to Cohen's terms is not at all inappropriate. Just as the amplification of a moral panic ultimately means all members of the deviant group are identified as threatening, so: 'an established group tends to attribute to its outsider group as a whole the "bad" characteristics of the group's "worst" section – of its anomic minority'. By contrast, 'the self-image of the established group tends to be modelled on its exemplary, most "nomic" or norm-setting section, on the minority of its "best" members' (Elias and Scotson 1994: xix). In other words, the outsiders, the folk devils, are tarred with the worst possible brush, whereas the established groups identify themselves as 'not like them' and, specifically, as most like those moral entrepreneurs (to recall the phrase of Becker and Cohen) who are able to establish rules. In the end the outsider groups themselves accept their 'badness'. For Cohen this can be the basis of a strategy of turning the tables on power whereby the folk devil revels in its deviance from social norms. But Elias sees the situation in rather more tragic terms:

> Attaching the label of "lower human value" to another group is one of the weapons used in a power struggle by superior groups as a means of maintaining their social superiority. In that situation the social slur cast by a more powerful upon a less powerful group usually enters

the self-image of the latter and, thus, weakens and disarms them.

(Elias and Scotson 1994: xxi)

According to Elias then, if you tell someone they are worthless and useless often enough they will not rebel. They will actually come to accept their evident lack of human value. After all, rebellion implies some vestige of a sense of self-worth.

But how are the established able to do this? Because they have monopolized the positions of power in the networks of interdependency. Precisely because they are the long-established participants they have cohesive social relationships which enable them to secure group control of the positions of power. This power is both institutional and less formal: 'because they had lived together for a fairly long time, the old families possessed as a group a cohesion which the newcomers lacked' (Elias and Scotson 1994: xxxviii). This sense of cohesion was of course enhanced in no small way by the initial lack of cohesion amongst the newcomers and by their failure to assume the positions of power (a failure that was largely inevitable given the extent to which the established group had control of institutions).

Outsiders then are outsiders precisely because they are excluded from the networks of interdependency in which the positions of power are monopolized by the established groups. The established justify this exclusion on the grounds of the lesser human value of the outsiders. The outsiders are people 'not like us', and their difference helps bolster what Elias calls the 'group charisma' of the established. Group charisma consists in the 'bonds of identification of individuals with their group and their participation by proxy in the collective attributes' (Elias and Scotson 1994: 103). Two conclusions follow from this claim. First, the analysis of folk devils and moral panics can be given a sociological depth it presently lacks as soon as it is appreciated how far it maps on to Elias's analysis of established-outsider figurations. Second, a measure of panic is actually necessary for established groups in order to reinforce their group charisma in the circumstances when it is being undermined by social change. The established and the outsiders are then caught in what Elias calls a 'double bind' (Elias and Scotson 1994: xxxi). The established need the outsiders to confirm the sense of virtue that is metaphysically unknowable yet sensed as being challenged by social change, and the outsiders seek moral and even material recognition from the established groups who otherwise withhold it. This implies a power balance that is permanently shifting, never stable. By extension it points to the inevitable fragility of all networks of interdependence. They are fragile because they involve power struggles.

There is something else about the folk devil that is worth pulling out. Their status as outsiders to the networks of interdependency is *symbolically represented by the spaces with which they are associated*. Think about where folk devils go about their activity. It's in impoverished housing estates, on beaches or nowadays often on the Internet. These are all *places on the margin*. They are not necessarily on the margin in the geographical sense, rather they are marginal in the sense of their positioning in cultural arrangements of space. To this extent the places where Cohen's Mods and Rockers went about their business – seaside resorts and beaches – were marginal both geographically and culturally. This is certainly true of Brighton, which has long had a reputation in Britain as the kind of place where anything goes, as Graham Greene saw (Shields 1991: 3). Folk devils rarely if ever are to be found 'at the centre' of networks. Instead they tend to occupy spaces that are culturally constructed as being marginal to the established networks of interdependency. They are outsiders not just because they are subject to the denigration of their human value. They are also outsiders because of the spaces they are forced to occupy.

Illustration of these points about folk devils and networks of interdependency can be found in the analysis of a moral panic in Australia which was carried out by Scott Poynting and two colleagues. Admittedly, it is necessary to read the evidence Poynting and his colleagues provide in a different way to how their own discussion reads it, but the connection to the themes I have been trying to develop is exact. They explore a moral panic about 'ethnic gangs' in the marginal space of an ethnically diverse yet traditionally working-class suburb of Sydney in 1998–2000. The panic followed from the murder of a 14-year-old Korean-Australian boy by a gang of Lebanese-Australian young men. The allegedly ethnic gangs were identified as outsiders to the established networks of interdependency. Their establishment as outsiders was possible because of the extent to which established groups had a dominant position in relationships of power. There were well-established and cohesive relationships between the local police, media and politicians (Poynting *et al.* 2001: 73, 85). The outsider-ness was represented in two ways. First, and perhaps most obviously, it was ethnicized. But second, it was also linked to expressions of masculinity which were seen as 'unAustralian'. Media and politicians alike noted how the young boy was stabbed to death. Knife carrying was immediately identified as an import from an alien culture (Poynting *et al.* 2001: 77). Underpinning all of this was rapid social change. The incident happened in a Sydney suburb that had been transformed:

> In a region with the demographics of contemporary Canterbury-Bankstown ... age and class relations are complicated by, and sometimes ideologically represented as, relations of ethnicity. The influx of migrants to these suburbs over the last two decades, and their age profile, means that many elderly Anglos, when confronted by youth, experience this as confrontation by *ethnic* youth.
> *(Poynting* et al. *2001: 77)*

Yet one thing all of this made possible was a reinforcement of the sense of the virtue of the established groups without the established, however, ever having to say in precisely what this virtue consisted. There was, 'the creation of a racialised Other:

> a "them" against whose "difference" a dominant national, ethnic "us" is defined. This entails the production of knowledge about this Other – a set of characteristics or behaviours, even a pathology – deployed to explain social and cultural difference, and to rationalise social exclusions.
> *(Poynting et al. 2001: 72)*

This is of course exactly where Elias's analysis would also point. In the case of the ethnic gangs of the Sydney suburb their pathology took the form of allegations of unAustralian ways of killing, a lack of respect for authority and a general unpredictability, a 'wildness'. Poynting and his colleagues go on to stress how this definition of 'us', 'involves the projection of anxieties about social problems onto the Other, which becomes seen as the cause of those problems, the source of conflict and disorder' (Poynting *et al.* 2001: 72).

Conclusion

If these points about folk devils are accepted, they can be linked to some comments by Ulrich Beck, and together they intimate a rather disturbing future. He has spoken about how young people in Europe, those who live in the marginal places of run-down estates, are now systemically excluded from the job market because inexperienced low-skilled labour (and young people are by definition inexperienced and low-skilled) has been outsourced. According to Beck: 'These people exist outside the job market, and society does not need them anymore: the economy can prosper without them, the governments can be elected without them' (Beck in Wimmer and Quandt 2006: 338). They are completely outside of the networks of interdependency and if Beck is right there is actually scarcely any likelihood of them ever being able to assert – or to be given – a way in. They are on the margins. They are indeed outsiders. Perhaps if Beck is right Eliasian themes need to be supplemented with recognition of the possibility of some groups being entirely excluded from networks of interdependency, except in as much as they can be vilified in order to shore up the fragile group charisma of the established.

So why are they folk devils? Because they are outsiders to the networks of interdependency, and the modern labour market makes sure there is no shortage of candidates for the role. They are also folk devils because they allow Colin Self's waiting women to go to their party, get drunk, and nevertheless believe in their own great virtue without having to bother with finding out what the word 'virtue' actually means.

3
PANIC AND TRUST

One of the set pieces in Don DeLillo's novel *White Noise* explores what the media quickly refer to as the 'airborne toxic event'. It's almost as if the template of the story was ready in advance of the event it ostensibly reported. A train crash released over the quiet university town of Blacksmith a cloud of what was said to be the lethal chemical Nyodene Derivative. This is the risk society come to the fictional Midwest. Once again art gets there first. Professor Jack Gladney, the non-German speaking founder of the local university's Department of Hitler Studies, is told to leave with his family. On the way to the abandoned scout camp to which everyone from his part of town is being evacuated Gladney has to fill the car with petrol. Despite everything, the infrastructure of modern life continues to function, just as Japanese trains still ran after the March 2011 tsunami. This brief period in the open air potentially left Gladney defenceless against the toxins in the air. But when screened by the emergency services Gladney was told he would have to wait fifteen years to know for sure what the effects might be, if indeed there actually would be any (DeLillo 1986: 164). Gladney had drawn the seeds of a later panic within his body and the collective panic has been personalized: 'The threat is perceived as immediate, not distant. In addition, the threat is perceived as ambiguous; its exact dimensions are not known' (Smelser 1962: 140). Still at least the threat of the toxins takes Gladney's mind away from dwelling too much on all the other ways he might come to die. This, the panic surrounding our death, is identified by DeLillo as the loudest of the many white noises by which we are presently assaulted.

When DeLillo describes the evacuation of the town he almost provides a case study of Smelser's account of panic and, specifically, how emergency services can manage it. The train crash has been the precipitating event, and the danger has been communicated by the media in increasingly dramatic yet actually more unintelligible ways (just as happened with the media coverage of Fukushima). What started as a 'feathery plume' soon became a 'black billowing cloud' (DeLillo 1986: 132) and then the blood-curdling 'airborne toxic event' (DeLillo 1986: 136). The residents of the town are all trying to escape before the cloud blows over their houses and, possibly, leaves a time-bomb of poison in their bodies. They're engaging in flight behaviour. But there is no panic in DeLillo's story. Or at least there is no panic in as much as it is linked with non-routine patterns of behaviour (DeLillo 1986: 141–2). Why not?

Smelser can give answers to the question. First of all, even though the route to the evacuation centre was jammed, there was still movement and, furthermore, everyone knew this was the main escape road. There was a way out which was kept open and, as Smelser discovered, one of the best ways of overcoming panic is for the authorities to make sure an escape route always remains available, regardless of the actual speed of travel (Smelser 1962: 138). Second, the authorities in DeLillo's story quickly gave unambiguous advice. They did not allow time for rumours to develop. Instead they took control of the definition of the situation (Smelser 1962: 159). This definition was one that stressed the *response* to the precipitating event rather than the toxic cloud itself. Admittedly the authorities in the story were not able to tell Gladney much about the death now maybe lurking within his body, but their message about the threat of Nyodene Derivative and what, therefore, needed to be done was always clear and consistent. The authorities told everyone to do what the authorities asked of them. Similarly, even as the media used words and images that amplified the dangers of the chemical, the message remained the same in substance if not in detail. The only doubt was *when not if* everyone would die of exposure unless they did what they were told. As Smelser showed, ambiguous information provokes anxiety and exacerbates the chances of panic (Smelser 1962: 141). Third, the authorities in *White Noise* assumed a leadership position. Based on their institutionally reinforced control of the definition of the situation they were able to provide a structure of meaning which to some degree normalized the extraordinary events of the toxic cloud and subsequent evacuation. No small part of the normalization was due to how the residents started to behave like evacuees who are seen on television. With this way of behaving, the evacuees, otherwise good affluent bourgeois Americans, became quietly compliant, just as institutions need them to be if they are to be able freely to act in terms of their own requirements of instrumental rationality. Put another way, Don DeLillo's story shows how institutionally reinforced authority can establish a recognizable network of interdependency in circumstances that might otherwise trigger panic. Institutions can achieve this when they all sing the same song loudly and relentlessly, and do not allow competing voices to be heard. For Smelser, 'divided authority, distrust of leaders, and so on' can be counted as 'high among the conditions that facilitate panic' (Smelser 1962: 162). It is noticeable how this distrust of leaders, and indeed differences in the information given by separate agencies, fed into what the media reported as the confused situation in Tokyo in the days after Fukushima. The Japanese authorities really ought to have taken into account DeLillo's fictional anticipation of their problems.

There are other themes to draw from DeLillo's story. I want to look at two of them. First, the story of the toxic cloud echoes to the sound of metaphysical panic mentioned in the previous chapter. It is worth quoting Smelser again. For him the precipitating event triggers panic because, 'it "confirms" the generalized suspicions and uneasiness of anxious people' (Smelser 1962: 147). Of course Smelser was not at all writing this comment with an eye to the level of metaphysics, but with this caveat in mind it nevertheless casts light. Gladney was certainly made anxious by his exposure to Nyodene Derivative. When he was told about the risk following from the time out of the car Gladney wondered: 'Death has entered. It is inside you.' But thanks to how this news is now communicated, through computers, X-rays and medical jargon,

> You are said to be dying and yet are separate from the dying, can ponder it at your leisure ... It is when death is rendered graphically, is televised so to speak, that you sense an eerie separation between your condition and yourself. In short: It makes you feel like a stranger in your own dying.
>
> *(DeLillo 1986: 165)*

The toxic cloud over Blacksmith illustrates the theme of metaphysical panic because, just like the bombing of Hiroshima and Nagasaki (but never forget: one example is fictional, another exceptionally actual), it shows how it is no longer possible to be certain. As the toxic event begins to unravel, Gladney objects to evacuating his house with all of its possessions. He believes evacuation at the behest of an external authority is something that happens to poor people living in trailers, and not to people like him, people like university professors. What he says anticipates what happened in New Orleans with Hurricane Katrina: 'These things happen to poor people who live in exposed areas. Society is set up in such a way that it's the poor and the uneducated who suffer the main impact of natural and man-made disasters' (DeLillo 1986: 133). Except of course it isn't any more. Education and income offer no defences against toxic clouds. Once upon a time Gladney might have been describing the situation very accurately when he said: 'I'm the head of a department. I don't see myself fleeing an airborne toxic event. That's for people who live in mobile homes out in the scrubby parts of the county, where the fish hatcheries are' (DeLillo 1986: 136–7). But no longer.

On the one hand this confirms Beck's point about how risk society is democratically blind to questions of social class and status. But on the other it also confirms suspicions about the fragility of the everyday. Nothing is immune from the acid of uncertainty. The situation is keenly felt by Jack Gladney's rather precociously clear-sighted son Heinrich. As soon as certain questions are asked they cannot be answered but neither can they be forgotten. Instead they continue to eat away at the foundations of confidence in the everyday. In the evening, sitting in the evacuation centre after being given food and drink, Heinrich looks around and sees what he calls the Stone Age:

> Here we are in the Stone Age, knowing all these great things after centuries of progress but what can we do to make life easier for the Stone Agers? Can we make a refrigerator? Can we even explain how it works? What is electricity? What is light?
>
> *(DeLillo 1986: 172)*

These are somewhat Weberian questions. As Max Weber pointed out, we all ride in 'streetcars' but most of us have absolutely no idea how they actually work. But Weber refused to go as far as Heinrich. Heinrich takes the questions to their shattering conclusion, whereas Weber desperately tried to cling on to the everyday. For Weber we do not need to ask how a car works. The modern man, 'is satisfied that he may "count" on the behavior of the streetcar, and he orients his conduct according to this expectation; but he knows nothing about what it takes to produce such a car so that it can move' (Weber 1948: 139). To ask these questions is to open up the abyss of metaphysical panic Weber tried so hard to avoid, but which DeLillo's fictional Heinrich resolutely confronts. For neither of them are there any definite answers, however.

There is a second theme to be drawn out of the incident of the airborne toxic event. It's a theme implicit to Weber's point about how we tend to take technology for granted, and ask no questions so long as it works. Like Weber's car travellers, DeLillo's residents were actually rather *trusting*. They did what the emergency services told them to do, and they were *dependent*. After all, 'What people in an exodus fear most immediately is that those in positions of authority will long since have fled, leaving us in charge of our own chaos' (DeLillo 1986: 140). People will trust those who assume control of the chaos. This is because in these kinds of situations, 'No one's knowledge is less secure than your own' (DeLillo 1986: 140). This is a point at which the fictional and the actual begin to leech into one another once again. Exactly the same thing happened in the aftermath of Fukushima. The Japanese authorities might have been discredited and social media might well have made the insecure opinions of anyone appear as valid as those of the experts, thus disturbing any chance of a single definition of the situation, but nevertheless people tended to do what they were asked to do. For instance people still queued to buy tickets to travel on trains and others still arrived early at the airport in order to go through check-in and security. Furthermore the distrust of authority was usually mixed up with implied pleas for institutions to get themselves sorted out and to begin to tell people what they ought to do for the best.

In the light of these observations this chapter explores whether *panic represents a breakdown in trust*. The exploration will proceed in two stages. First of all the meaning of trust will be established, and it will be shown how breakdowns in trust can be identified as the sociological cause of the distinctly contemporary phenomenon of the fear of flying. The second part of the chapter explores some popular psychological and sociological literature about how the breakdown of trust generates a sense of self-hood which has to see itself as if from a distance if it is going to be able to survive the troubles of these times. To this extent the chapter is also concerned to identify aspects of the panicking – or indeed non-panicking – self.

What is trust?

According to Anthony Giddens, trust is a defining feature of contemporary social life. This is because our lives and activities are dominated by expert systems – systems that can be as banal as the design of a refrigerator – about which most of us have no knowledge (for example could you repair a broken kitchen appliance?) and which have no necessary and intrinsic ties to time and place. The refrigerator in my kitchen might well have been designed in America or Germany or Korea, but I do not know, and more importantly I feel no need to find out, so long as it continues to work. I trust the manufacturers and, ultimately, I trust in the technology. I have *trust* rather than complete *certainty* because the activity of the manufacturers, and indeed the operation of the appliance, is invisible to me. I can't see or understand what they do, so I trust they have done it properly. The continuous operation of the appliance is the justification for my trust.

> So how does Giddens define trust? He says it, 'may be defined as confidence in the reliability of a person or system, regarding a given set of outcomes or events, where that confidence expresses a faith in the probity or love of

> another, or in the correctness of abstract principles (technical knowledge).
>
> *(Giddens 1990: 34)*

The word 'faith' rather leaps out of the definition of trust. Indeed, for Giddens there is a close connection of trust with faith, and ultimately trust actually *is* a kind of faith: 'Trust is inevitably in part an article of "faith" … There is a pragmatic element in "faith," based upon the experience that such systems generally work as they are supposed to do' (Giddens 1990: 29). But it is necessary to avoid too much slippage between the two terms, and so Giddens says: 'Trust is not the same as faith in the reliability of a person or system; it is what derives from that faith' (Giddens 1990: 33).

These definitions reflect a debt Giddens owes to the discussion of money offered in the early twentieth century by Georg Simmel. Money in fact provides an excellent example of trust in contemporary social relationships. Quite simply, money only 'works' as a means of buying and selling things because there is a shared trust in the value of the paper, credit or electronic transaction. Without this kind of trust the economy would collapse (Simmel 1990: 179). Central banks underpin this trust. They guarantee the value of the money by linking it to gold reserves or, in these days when the amount of money in the global economic system has very far outstripped the amount of gold, their ability to guarantee sovereign debt. When this trust in central banks breaks down money becomes worthless. To some degree this is what happened in Greece in 2011. As Simmel saw, such trust requires a measure of faith:

> It expresses the feeling that there exists between our idea of a being and the being itself a definite connection and unity, a certain consistency in our conception of it, an assurance and lack of resistance in the surrender of the Ego to this conception.
>
> *(Simmel 1990: 179)*

Money has value because the idea of it is connected through an act of a kind of faith to the very substance of value (gold or institutional probity), and when this connection is pragmatically validated – as it is every time money is used – the self simply accepts it.

Giddens also talks about trust and money, but he is more interested in trust in relation to technological systems. These systems highlight the extent to which contemporary life is dependent on things that are actually not understood. However, this lack of understanding can be overcome by a faith in the expertise of designers and, indeed, on one's own instrumental skills. Giddens gives the example of a car. The situation has moved on from Weber's quiet passengers, and now we are not just the riders, we are the drivers. But we only drive because we have trust. According to Giddens, when I

> get into a car, I enter settings which are thoroughly permeated by expert knowledge – involving the design and construction of automobiles, highways, intersections, traffic lights, and many other items. Everyone knows that driving a car is a dangerous activity, entailing the risk of accident. In choosing to go out in the car, I accept that risk, but rely upon the aforesaid expertise to guarantee that it is minimised as far as possible.
>
> *(Giddens 1990: 28)*

But perhaps the clearest example Giddens gives of trust in systems concerns flying in a plane. As he points out:

> A person can board a plane in London and reach Los Angeles some ten hours later and be fairly certain that not only will the journey be made safely, but that the plane will arrive quite close to a predetermined time.
>
> *(Giddens 1990: 112)*

This is even though the passenger (someone like you and I) doesn't know how it all works. Experience underpins a pragmatic faith in the arrival of the plane in the right place at the right time, and so there is a high level of trust in the system. All of this comes together in what Giddens calls *ontological security,* a 'sense of the reliability of persons and things' (Giddens 1990: 92).

Now it is possible to relate the discussion of trust to the definition of panic upon which this book builds. Panic has been defined as *confrontation with the fragility of the complexity upon which daily routine is dependent.* Complexity is a product of the extent to which social relationships are now impossible without participation in networks of interdependency. By extension then, trust can be defined as the sense of the solidity of these networks. The trust is *ontological* in as much as it relates to the experience of being in the world, and the sense of security follows from, 'the confidence that most human beings have in the continuity of their self-identity and in the constancy of the surrounding social and material environments of action' (Giddens 1990: 92). Therefore *panic is the sense of insecurity, lack of confidence and, in all, the collapse of trust, which is caused when the 'social and material environments of action' can no longer be accepted as constant and inevitable because of the impact of a risk event or a disorderly social event.*

On this basis it is possible to offer a hypothesis: *when there is a loss of trust in a network of interdependency, or as Giddens would have it, an 'environment of action', it will tend to occasion more panic than previously in so far as the network has become unavoidable.* This hypothesis is justified by what happened to the incidence of the fear of flying after 9/11.

As we have seen Giddens used flying as a way of illustrating his claims about trust. When we fly on an aeroplane we are demonstrating in a very practical way our trust in expert systems about which we are likely to have little or no knowledge (Giddens 1990: 28). But there is more. There is also trust because the abstract system is personalized and made routine by the attitude displayed by air crews. If Giddens is right, and the claim does seem to be perfectly valid, the tendency of pilots and cabin crew always to show a calm and relaxed professionalism is itself designed, just like the technology of the plane, to generate trust. As he puts it: 'the studied casualness and calm cheer of air crew personnel are probably as important in reassuring passengers as any number of announcements demonstrating statistically how safe air travel is' (Giddens 1990: 86). Don DeLillo got there first. One chapter in *White Noise* tells about Gladney waiting for his daughter at the airport, but seeing instead a group of dishevelled passengers coming through Arrivals. The plane had lost altitude and the passengers thought they were about to die. DeLillo describes the panic on the flight but how, once the engines fired back into life, the passengers quickly calmed down, thanks to one of the flight crew: 'The first officer walked down the aisle, smiling and chatting in an empty pleasant corporate way. His face had the rosy and confident polish that is familiar in handlers of large passenger aircraft' (DeLillo 1986: 109). In a case of life imitating art in April 2012 a flight from Italy to the UK lost altitude when the cabin depressurized over the Alps. People started to become terrified but the cabin crew reacted professionally and as if everything was under complete control. Evidently the terror lessened because of their calmness. The plane safely landed at Frankfurt instead of the East Midlands (Meikle 2012).

However the attitude emphasized by DeLillo and Giddens underwent something of a change after 9/11. In particular Amy L. Fraher has explored increasing pressure amongst American commercial airline pilots to be allowed to carry hand guns when they are flying. The obvious reason why the pilots wanted to carry guns was, of course, to reduce the chances of a 9/11-style takeover of the controls. Quite simply with a hand gun you can shoot the terrorist, although this rather leaves hanging the question of what would happen if you missed and punctured the shell of the plane instead. Furthermore, this desire to carry hand guns belies the 'calm cheer' that Giddens identified in flight crews. You only need to carry a gun if you don't trust the other people you might meet in your 'environment of action'. But Fraher discovered a lot more. Pilots wanted to carry guns because this enabled them to maintain the role of the heroic individual which she found was important to their sense of self. This role had been undermined by 9/11 itself, but also by the subsequent economic problems of the airline industry and, curiously, the need for airline pilots to undergo more strenuous security screening before boarding a plane than baggage handlers. The pilots experienced a 'sense of loss of trustworthiness' which, 'combined with their valencies to play the hero led to the laudable, though misguided, effort to satisfy unrealistic expectations projected by the American public' (Fraher 2004: 590). Indeed:

> Pilots used phantasy and illusion at work in an effort to overcome the post-traumatic stress and difficulties arising from their sense of shame for not stopping the hijackings, guilt about the crashes and personal fear of death at the hands of terrorists.
>
> *(Fraher 2004: 591)*

In short pilots wanted to take guns to work in order to try to keep their own panic, their own sense of ontological insecurity, at bay.

The situation is rather different for passengers. Since 9/11 and plots to blow up planes in mid-flight, security checks have become increasingly intrusive. According to one more than a little sensationalist British newspaper report body scanners being tested at American airports can look through clothing to underwear and, it was hinted, even a little further (*Daily Mail* 2009). Whether or not this is true is largely besides the point. What is important about this story is what it says about trust. The maintenance of physical security has become incompatible with the maintenance of ontological security, and every plane passenger is treated as a potential cause of panic. Passengers are unable to be heroic individuals and so they become even more dependent upon the pilot who, if Fraher's study is anything to go by, does not trust the passengers. This curious situation probably explains the appeal of films like *United 93*, which identify passengers as the heroes of 9/11. Such films are consoling fantasies, even though they are based on 'true events'.

According to a poll taken in November 2001, 43 per cent of Americans were 'somewhat afraid' of flying, and another 17 per cent were 'very afraid' (Stoller 2006). Flight ticket sales were significantly lower on 9/11 2002 and 2003 than in previous years or on either September 10 or 12. An American press report said:

> In 2002, airlines cut already reduced flight schedules in anticipation of the anniversary, and some airports reported that traffic was down as much as 50 percent on the day itself. The low-cost carrier Spirit Airlines went so far as to offer free flights to those brave or stingy enough to take a chance. More planes took off on Sept. 11, 2003, but still not as many as usual.
>
> *(Oremus 2011)*

Passenger air miles decreased quickly after 9/11. In October, November and December 2001 they were 20 per cent, 17 per cent and 12 per cent respectively lower than the same month one year previously (Gigerenzer 2004: 286). Miriam Tucker, an American journalist, reported on her own increased fear of flying after 9/11. She knew flying remained far safer than car driving, and yet the situation seemed to be the other way round. Why? Because after 9/11 the media kept reporting stories about, 'Security breaches, unruly passengers, Congress's urgent pursuit of an airline security bill, and of course, the terrible crash of Flight 587 in New York' (Tucker 2001; American Airlines Flight 587 from JFK to the Dominican Republic crashed shortly after take-off on 12 November 2001; 260 people on the plane died, and another five on the ground). Clearly, people became more fearful about flying in the wake of 9/11. On this basis there appears to be good reason to postulate a more or less temporary spike in the incidence of flight-related panic attacks due to the risk event of the terrorist attacks. Indeed trust collapsed in the face of 'discussions of airline safety, anthrax, and potential threats, as well as criticism of agencies for not acting expeditiously' (Kormos 2003: 145).

The American Psychiatric Association's *Diagnostic and Statistical Manual of Mental Disorders* defines the fear of flying as a clinically identifiable phobia. It usually expresses itself as a fear of crashing, fear of confined spaces, height and the sense of a lack of control (Newgent *et al.* 2006: 28). Put another way the fear of flying is also a fear of individual powerlessness and of absolute dependency. The fear of flying might therefore be identified as a distillation of the panics generated by the implication of the individual in complex networks of interdependency. But since the fear of flying is identified as a clinical condition, unsurprisingly it is pretty much exclusively discussed in terms of its treatment and psychological intervention with individuals who present to psychologists and psychiatric professionals.

One study reports the case of Jennifer, and explicitly addresses the impact of 9/11. Although Jennifer was able to take flights, she did not do so often, and when she did she found the experience to be quite uncomfortable, evidently because of extreme feelings of a lack of control (Newgent *et al.* 2006: 32). Jennifer's stress levels were reduced by undergoing a brief period of counselling and desensitization treatment. She was able to take 24 flights without any undue panic. This was before 9/11. Jennifer then reported a rise in her stress levels but, thanks to the panic-control measures she had learned in counselling, she quickly became able to fly again. Indeed: 'Jennifer reported that she felt empowered when flying after September 11 and that she felt she could act if something went wrong' (Newgent *et al.*

2006: 33). Her counsellors were certain they had discovered, 'an efficient and successful treatment for nontraumatic fear of flying' which 'empowers' the likes of Jennifer to 'help themselves' (Newgent *et al.* 2006: 34). Another report concerns the case of G.L., a 28-year-old German who's fear of flying was now getting in the way of his ability to do his job. He was convinced the plane he was taking would crash because of a mid-air collision or mechanical failure (Kormos 2003: 146). G.L. was subjected to a course of treatment which desensitized his fear through exposure to it. This method was chosen because, 'it takes less time and is more cost-effective' (Kormos 2003: 146). The treatment was successful. G.L. became able to take flights whenever his job demanded and his career started to advance. It would seem this report discusses a treatment that was implemented before 9/11, but it was taken by the author to speak directly to the new world:

> Since September 11, 2001, the mental health professional will play a more visible role in primary care and the public health arena. There will be a greater need for programs to educate primary care physicians, nurses, and the community at large to recognize the symptoms of mood and anxiety disorders.
>
> *(Kormos 2003: 150)*

The author of this particular report was a clinical health nurse working in private practice in St Louis.

If these reports are read through the prism of the discussion of trust they become very interesting sociologically. Let's take the reports at face value. They are both about a debilitating collapse of the sense of ontological security, of the trust, which two individuals had been required by their jobs or lifestyles to invest in complex technological systems. This collapse was due to the individual's own lack of understanding of expert knowledge. So 9/11 was a moment that could have precipitated panic – as it did for Fraher's airline pilots – but thanks to clinical interventions this did not happen. In short, therapeutic intervention enabled both Jennifer and G.L. to recover a sense of the reliability of the people and things in their routine daily lives (to recall Giddens's definition of ontological security). They were able not to panic. But how were Jennifer and G.L. so able? This is where the 'empowering' story of the reports reveals a subtext. The counselling essentially taught Jennifer and G.L. not to trust in themselves but, instead, to trust in the systems. They were both encouraged to accept their complete dependency on complex networks over which, as Jennifer and G.L. both saw very clearly, they had no control but which they simply could not avoid. Their sense of ontological security was recovered through an acceptance of dependency. The situation compares with Jack Gladney's family in the evacuation centre, only able to eat and drink what and when the emergency services decided. Consequently 'helping yourself' to overcome fears actually means 'trust others and not yourself'.

What self?

The message is reinforced by the wider body of popular psychology literature about panic. According to much – if not all – of this literature, panic is something we all experience. It is normal, but it creeps up on us unnoticed. Consequently it is impossible for us entirely to trust ourselves because actually we do not know for sure what is going to happen next. We have to learn lessons taught by others. We have to allow ourselves to be dependent.

The author of one popular book, Áine Tubridy, puts it this way: 'Panic ... can occur on a day when you are relaxing, or on your holidays, when you figure you are not worrying about anything, or in the shower, or even in bed!' (Tubridy 2003: viii). Panic saps our ability to trust in ourselves. It can happen, 'without warning' leaving people, 'incredulous, shocked, shaken and utterly mystified as to what has just happened' (Tubridy 2003: 8). For Tubridy, panic creates terror because it seems to take control of the individual, leaving them experiencing the attack as little more than a passenger taking a ride they neither asked for nor enjoy (Tubridy 2003: 115). The parallel with the fear of flying is quite clear. Furthermore, just as Don DeLillo discussed how medical and computer technology makes the individual something like a spectator on their own death, the viewer of a television programme in which they are both murderer and victim, so panic is established by Tubridy as an emotional condition making life something that happens to us rather than something we do of our own volition. According to Tubridy panic can, however, be tackled and in the end even taken under control if we develop what she calls a 'toolbox of skills' we might use as and when necessary (Tubridy 2003: 115). We need to become the emergency engineers of our own anxieties. And in much the same way as an engineer takes a long hard look at the mechanism before deciding how to mend it, we must do the same to ourselves. Tubridy says we can deal with panic if we can learn to become *witnesses* to ourselves:

> A witness is someone who "looks at something happening". It implies standing back and looking from a distance ... By developing the ability to become a witness to your panic attacks as they happen, to pull back and see what's happening from a more objective position, you can get a lot of useful information.
>
> *(Tubridy 2003: 121)*

It then becomes possible to take the tools out of their box and repair the machine quickly and effectively. But in order to achieve this it is necessary '*not to resist what is happening*' (Tubridy 2003: 122; original emphasis).

A similar story can be found in another piece of popular psychology, this time by Christine Ingham. Whereas Tubridy positioned herself as a medical professional trying to understand and offer ways of coping with an illness, Ingham positions herself as someone who has suffered panic attacks but learned to turn them around, from fear to usefulness. Consequently Ingham's book is offered in the spirit of self-help and empowerment. She says her first panic attack was 'devastating' and the second 'terrifying'. This was because Ingham stopped being able to trust in herself. Panic told her she didn't really know herself. It showed Ingham she was an alien to herself:

> when you have panic attacks you gradually begin to tiptoe through each hour, every day, wary lest you disturb that sleeping monster and nudge it into life again; the one which makes you quake with fear and trembling in front of its gnashing and awful jaws.
>
> *(Ingham 2000: 3)*

Like Tubridy, Christine Ingham outlines ways to control panic attacks, and then she goes a step further. She doesn't just want us to overcome panic attacks by using a box of tools. Rather Ingham advocates turning panic around, learning why and when it happens and thus transforming it into a positive force for self-knowledge. For Ingham if we stop panicking when we panic we can look the monster in the eye and learn what it is trying to tell us about ourselves. As with Tubridy then, Ingram wants us to be able to look at ourselves as if from the outside.

These kinds of arguments make it hard not to return to the sociology of Anthony Giddens. What Tubridy and Ingham both advocate amounts to a *reflexive project of the self* wherein, 'self-identity is constituted by the reflexive ordering of self-narratives' (Giddens 1991: 244). In this definition the word 'reflexivity' points to self-knowledge and understanding. Giddens sees it as an intrinsic part of contemporary social life: 'individuals must become used to filtering all sorts of information relevant to their life situations and routinely act on the basis of that

Panic and trust **83**

filtering process'. This is because, 'individuals more or less have to engage with the wider world if they are to survive in it' (Giddens 1994: 6–7). Consequently the self is a reflexive project when previous events (such as a panic attack) are identified as effects with causes. When the causes are identified the effect (the panic attack) can be understood and the individual can assume greater self-knowledge. Reflexivity means the ability to tell stories (create ordering self-narratives) which situate the self in a present which has a past from which lessons have been learned and a future which can be the opportunity for ever-better self-knowledge. For Giddens, 'A person's identity is not to be found in behaviour, nor – important though this is – in the reactions of others, but in the capacity *to keep a particular narrative going*' (Giddens 1991: 54)[1]. By this definition then, panic attacks as understood by Tubridy and Ingham are terrifying precisely because they demolish the ability of the self to 'keep a particular narrative going'. The attacks destroy the self, but for Tubridy and Ingham this situation can be used to good effect so long as the right tools are available, and if the panic is seen as a learning experience. As such their solution to panic is to use it as a spur to revise and yet continue with a narrative of the self.

This is how the popular psychology of panic, and indeed Giddens's sociology of reflexivity, would wish to see the situation. They all accept the challenges of living in the contemporary world with its complex networks and technological systems. None of them pretend it is easy. But nevertheless, they all suggest, the individual can recover and maintain a coherent sense of self if she or he learns to take control of the situation by imposing a different narrative upon it, a narrative that has been written in the first instance thanks to lessons taught by others. But what can taking control possibly mean? Neither Tubridy, Ingham nor Giddens actually suggests a *changing* of the situation. All they stress is a new narrative about the situation, and so the situation itself becomes an external context as opposed to an 'environment of action' which can be influenced just as it influences. What they suggest is *reflexivity* about the situation: thinking about it and, ultimately, seeing it as a cognitive rather than practical issue. Christine Ingham takes the position to its logical conclusion when she advocates being positive about a situation which is itself confronted as simply 'there' and never in terms of any possibility of an alternative. This is a popular psychology of quietism.

It is also a popular psychology of trivialization. For Tubridy and Ingham even mundane activities like taking a shower or going to bed can bring about a collapse of trust in the self. Furthermore, even though Giddens's point about how we become dependent on expert systems every time we open the car door or travel on a plane is correct, these are also completely normal and routine practices nowadays. Giddens is right but his way of making the point minimizes its significance and insight. On the one hand this actually dissolves the possibility of panic in as much as panic, following Smelser, is the effect of exceptional causal events. Now it can be caused by plumbing and an ignition key. On the other hand the attitude of the likes of Tubridy, Ingham and indeed Giddens actually transforms the meaning of the self. It stops being a reflexive agent of its own constitution, and instead it becomes the survivor of the supposedly most dangerous environment, the environment of the mundane everyday. Certainly in Tubridy and Ingham there is a sense of the self being under attack and in urgent need of ways of defending itself from the panic that might break out anywhere and everywhere. This is a trivialization that 'testifies to a pervasive sense of danger – to a perception that nothing, not even the simplest domestic detail, can be taken for granted' (Lasch 1984: 62; the first and third parts of DeLillo's *White Noise* are incisive explorations of what it means to live in a world in which even simple domestic details are potentially infused with danger). Now the cause of panic has shifted from the event to the sense of the self.

What kind of self? Quite possibly not the reflexive self of Giddens. A far more provocative picture is painted by Christopher Lasch. Writing in the 1980s and with his eye on the American experience, but in a way remaining exceptionally prescient, he identified these as 'troubled times'. He had earlier shown in what these 'troubles' consist: 'Defeat in Vietnam, economic stagnation, and the impending exhaustion of natural resources' (Lasch 1979: xiii). The list can be updated to cover a lack of a definite outcome in Iraq and Afghanistan, economic decline relative to China, peak oil and, a new item, recognition of the side effects of technological systems (Beck's *Risk Society*, DeLillo's *White Noise*). In these times, everyday life becomes a demanding environment of action which is confronted as something needing to be survived. As Lasch said we live as if the great disaster has already happened and: 'We conduct ourselves as if we lived in "impossible circumstances", in an "apparently irresistible environment", in the "extreme and immutable environment" of the prison or the concentration camp' (Lasch 1984: 95). Or indeed in the shower or in bed. This sense of the world leads to a kind of self-hood that retreats from commitments and lives very much in the moment, in order to overcome the small everyday obstacles. It is a self living in the trees not the forest. The immediate present is as threatening to the self as a nuclear power station, and by confronting its obstacles it is possible to 'function' (Lasch 1984: 96). The resonance with the arguments of Tubridy and Ingham, even Giddens, is clear.

According to Lasch, and directly contrary to Giddens, the self who seeks to survive these troubled times is not at all tied to a concern to 'keep a narrative going'. Rather, Lasch says, the life of the contemporary survivor-self, 'consists of isolated acts and events. It has no story, no pattern, no structure of an unfolding narrative. The decline of the narrative mode ... reflects the fragmentation of the self' (Lasch 1984: 96). By Lasch's argument, then, narratives have collapsed because the self cannot be tied down or, indeed, allow her or himself to be distracted by any vision that is beyond the immediate present. After all, here and now has to be survived, and worrying about the past or the future can therefore be dangerous. This is a kind of sensibility that is advocated in the literature about the fear of flying. The lesson is always to forget the past, not worry about the future, and instead focus only on the present moment. But this in turn raises another aspect of the self in troubled times.

What kind of focus is practised in this ongoing present? It's a kind that is, once again, almost perfectly illustrated by the counselling and popular psychology literature. The self understands itself to be having to survive troubled times, and Lasch says: 'Survivors have to learn the trick of observing themselves as if the events of their lives were happening to someone else.' He goes on to explain how the collapse of a sense of the narrative self is due to how in these times individuals,

> no longer see themselves as subjects at all but rather as the victims of circumstance, and this feeling of being acted on by uncontrollable external forces prompts another mode ... a withdrawal from the beleaguered self into the person of a detached, bemused, ironic observer.
> *(Lasch 1984: 96)*

Or, as Tubridy would have it, a withdrawal into the person of a *witness*. Or, as Giddens might have it, the self as a reflexive project, perpetually monitoring itself.

The temper of Lasch's discussion is quite different to the temper of the popular psychology. The latter sees panic as an inevitable quality of contemporary life which can, however, be overcome and indeed turned to good functional–instrumental use if it can be seen properly. This requires a kind of self capable of seeing itself from a distance or, to use a different analogy, a kind of self capable of seeing itself as a mechanism distinct from the mechanic. Lasch implies something very different. If his discussion is pursued panic is generated by these troubled times, and yet the burden can be borne by a kind of self-hood which tactically retreats from the world and which, furthermore, celebrates its ability simply to survive. This self disengages from the world (Lasch 1984: 98), in exactly the way the popular psychology advocates and, moreover, in a way that is remarkably close to the desensitization techniques advocated in the studies of the fear of flying. Consequently this self becomes more concerned with the inner life than the outer, with the personal not the public. Only in this way can the self become healthy enough to take flights even in the knowledge of the possibility of terrorist attacks. The visual representation of this self is the person in the queue at an airport or train station wearing a face mask. The mask is meant to keep the toxins out, but it also demolishes the chance for face-to-face social engagement between strangers. The mask is a barrier between the self – who can feel her or his own warm breath – and everything outside which is treated with a cold aloofness.

'The successful patient has learned to withdraw from the painful tension of assent and dissent in his relation to society by relating himself more affirmatively to his depths', said Philip Rieff in his eye-opening analysis of contemporary culture and self-hood. He went on to say of the 'patient' of the sort who has been successfully counselled, and who has been able to learn how to handle the tools in the box given by popular psychology: 'His newly acquired health entails a self-concern that takes precedence over social concern and encourages an attitude of ironic insight on the part of the self toward all that is not self.' For Rieff this means an ability to manage in the world purchased with the price of inward 'alienation' (Rieff 1960: 330). At this point it is worth recalling the argument of Dostoevsky's Ivan Karamazov which was discussed in the previous chapter. According to those who summarized his views Ivan Karamazov saw the rise of egoism 'even to the point of evildoing' thanks to the collapse of a belief in immortality. Such a collapse is indeed implied by the emergence of these 'troubled times' and it is more than coincidentally how the Dostoevskian claim fits with the arguments of Lasch and Reiff. The egoistic self which Dostoevsky bewailed has in contemporary culture taken the form of a self disengaged from the world in order to survive, a self for whom the inner depths are far more important than anything outside, a self for whom the ability to function in everyday life is a minor success story. It is a self who panics when its own survival is threatened but who trusts in counsellors and psychologists enough to let them teach lessons on how to withdraw from a world for which there is allegedly no alternative. It is Lasch's minimal self, the Prometheus of panic in the shower room.

Conclusion

Something at once understandable and odd happened after 9/11. In America, at least, people started to drive instead. In particular there was a significant increase in the number of long-distance journeys on interstate highways (Gigerenzer 2004: 286). This is understandable: 9/11 was a precipitating event for a collapse of trust in abstract technological systems. Consequently people turned to another technical system – cars and highways – but one that became more trustworthy precisely because it is immune to 9/11-type incidents. Furthermore driving a car gives the individual more control over their environment than they can have sitting in a plane. If something goes wrong with a plane the non-expert passenger can do absolutely nothing, but anyone can pull over if a tyre punctures or a car windscreen breaks. Anyone with a modicum of fairly basic knowledge can refuel a car. From a sociological point of view, the turn from the plane to the car also fits in with Lasch's minimal self. The new drivers were responding to troubled times by finding a way of continuing to function whilst at the same time retreating as far as possible into their own ostensibly safe and secure, panic-free, private worlds. They became survivors. Well, most of them did. Perhaps unsurprisingly, as the number of car journeys increased, so did the number of road fatalities. According to what appears to the non-expert to be a robust statistical analysis, the increase in road traffic after 9/11 caused an additional 350 deaths on the highways of the United States. 266 people died in the planes on 9/11 (Gigerenzer 2004: 287).

This is where the odd thing kicks in. There was and has been no panic about the increase in road deaths. Now this could well be because 9/11 was such a massive catastrophic event it managed to swamp everything else. But maybe it's also because the victims of motoring accidents died as individuals and not as members of a collective. They were in their own cars, hiding from a troubling world, rather than in the collective space of a plane and thereby putting themselves at the front of confrontation with these times. Consequently the message to be drawn from the increase in road fatalities could actually be construed as comforting for those who did not crash. First of all, the very fact of their avoidance of fatality could be taken as sufficient proof of their possession of enhanced survival skills. Second, it confirmed the need to withdraw even further into the self – so even the minimal self might come to seem a little too big – because obviously you can't trust other road users. And since these road users are neighbours, workmates and possibly even lovers, the message is ultimately: trust no one.

CONCLUSION

The Introduction to this book proposed the following hypothesis: *the confrontation with fragility is the sociological cause of panic*. Fragility is a quality of the extremely complex networks of interdependency upon which contemporary social relationships are reliant and without which these very relationships would be impossible. The book has been concerned to offer some ways of thinking through and with the hypothesis. In the first chapter the discussion focused on how the confrontation with fragility is caused by the sudden occurrence of a more or less *catastrophic risk event*. The 2011 failure of the Fukushima nuclear plant in Japan offered a case study of the risk event. In the second chapter the discussion moved on to think about confrontation with fragility because of the *disorderly social event*. These disorderly events are said to be carried out by folk devils and they cause moral panics. But what folk devils have in common, seemingly from time to time and place to place, is how they are identified as outsiders to an established, institutionalized, order which is confronting change. The third chapter looked at panic from the point of view of trust. Panic is what happens when trust breaks down. Risk events and disorderly social events are situations in which trust has indeed collapsed. Trust is about confidence in the durable solidity and strength of the things upon which we depend. Consequently when these things are shown to be fragile they cannot be trusted anymore, or at least not until they are strengthened again.

The discussion has necessarily paid a lot of attention to the centrality of the media in the communication, creation and shaping of panic. Risk events are imperceptible, and before the signs of danger have become obvious they can only be known because of the media. Even then the signs are not necessarily accepted as self-evident, as the debate about climate change shows. Meanwhile disorderly social events (moral panics) are often media amplifications of what was in the first instance a fairly singular occurrence. For example, Australians have worried about a spate of knife crime because of the amplification of one admittedly terrible incident. But this does not at all mean *reducing* panic to the media. Instead it means putting the media into their wider social context. Although panic is impossible without the media, the media are *not* the *sufficient* explanation for panic. This is one of the main points this little book wants to stress. Just like panic, the media need to be understood sociologically.

The book's discussion has not been guided by an attempt to *prove* or to *validate* the hypothesis with which it began. The hypothesis was offered with a different intention, as a hopefully useful way of *orienting thought*. The material in each of the three chapters can be best read as explorations of insights that the hypothesis opens up. To make this claim obviously begs questions: What insights have opened up, if any? What has been revealed about panic?

Smelser saw panic as a collective flight from established behaviour in order to preserve lives, property and power from the threat caused by a specific precipitating event (Smelser 1962: 131). By Smelser's definition, when there is not panic everything is calm and the established ways of going on in the world just carry on. Panic, therefore, is an aberration from the orderly norm. This book has painted panic on a broader canvas. Certainly Smelser is absolutely right to specify panic as unusual. After all if panic were commonplace it would lose its specificity and actually not be panic. It would be fear or anxiety instead. But the thread of panic is woven into the fabric of the complex networks of interdependency. Unusual yes, an aberration no. In other words, panic is not a visitor from outside. Rather it is an immanent possibility within contemporary social life. All the time life is dependent on complexity there is the possibility of panic precisely because complex systems are always closer to the edge of fragility than simpler ones. For instance many things could go wrong between me typing these words and you reading them, but if we were in the same room together, if the communication between us were simpler, it would be able to withstand any number of challenges. As a relationship in which we are dependent on one another as either speaker or listener our conversation would be far more robust, far less fragile. Indeed, and recalling the point from Walter Benjamin which was made at the end of the first chapter, if we were in the same room we would be able to share humanly meaningful stories about the world of our dependency and interdependency rather than just receive information from the media (and the media are themselves agents of complication and complexity).

The institutionalized order of what Smelser calls 'established patterns of behaviour' makes the complex interdependencies appear to be natural and evidently 'the way things must be'. Institutions give solidity to the otherwise fragile (and indeed to what these institutions have the power to say would be fragile without the prop they proclaim they provide). Consequently, the institutionalized order can also be identified as the guarantor of ontological security where security means maintenance of trust in the status quo. This lends durability to networks of interdependency. It's the durability of longevity and evident roots. The networks are certainly made durable in relation to any given individual towards whom they are indifferent. Therefore the networks evidently justify a high degree of trust. All of this is what the precipitating event of a panic undermines. On this basis it is possible to suggest:

> *As confrontation with the fragility of complexity, panic is a realization of ontological insecurity. And in as much as panic is a realization of insecurity, the routine solution to panic is the reinforcement of the institutions which are identified as the guarantors of ontological security.*

Giddens's phrase 'ontological security' clarifies panic as the sudden awareness, thanks to a risk event or disorderly social event, of the extent to which institutionally naturalized 'environments of action' are not as trustworthy as their routine acceptance implies. Furthermore the nub of panic is not just, as Smelser would have it, a matter of preservation. It is more broadly a desire for things to be stable. In other words ontological security is also about predictability. What is predictable is what is trusted, and what is trusted is what is predictable. Predictability has two aspects. First it means routine action over time, as in the case of a car which always works when the ignition key is turned. Second it means a definite connection linking appearance with substance, as in the case of Simmel's understanding of money which was mentioned in Chapter 3.

Through the prism of panic it is possible to identify four strands to contemporary ontological security. *First* of all, and perhaps most fundamentally, security involves a stress on the durability and predictability of the physical environment. This is both the environment of the body and the environment in which the body is situated. It can be seen by negation in the panics that surround invisible radiation, the threat of violence, the fear of flying, global viruses and so on. This is the level at which Smelser's discussion of panic primarily operates.

Similarly Beck's discussion of risk society largely focuses on the question of the physical environment. *Second*, security involves a stress on the instrumentality of institutions. Institutions are trusted all the time they are identified as operating predictably according to their own instrumentality and most certainly without regard to persons. The owners of the Fukushima plant were vilified when it became possible to see some of the problems at the power station as the result of deliberate cost-cutting in the pursuit of profit. The purported instrumentality of institutions lends them credibility as durable agents capable of dealing objectively with risk events. *Third*, ontological security involves a stress on the durable social order which is based on the naturalized and routine acceptance of networks of interdependency. The social order is also, moreover, made more predictable than it otherwise might be by rule-making and rule-enforcing institutions. This strand of ontological security is known, on the one hand, by the possibility of leading a life of no surprises and, on the other, by negation, through the disdain directed at outsiders as folk devils. They are the reminders of all the unpredictable things we ought not to be and indeed cannot be if others are to depend on us as we depend on them. *Fourth*, and at the grandest level, ontological security consists in a focus entirely and exclusively on the things of this world in order to divert attention from the abyss of metaphysical panic. It is worth recalling Colin Self's painting of the waiting women which was discussed in Chapter 2. At least the flight of the bombers and oblivion of one kind or another is predictable.

Panic is about the need of men and women confronting the fragility of complexity to find something predictable in which to trust. As soon as the point is put this way, it is possible to clarify the most significant question the book raises: Why can't we trust ourselves and one another instead?

This Conclusion starts with an exploration of the question why we don't just trust ourselves and one another. In its first part the discussion returns to the work of Christopher Lasch which was mentioned in the previous chapter. He offers a way of thinking about what kind of people we are, what kind of social characters we have. In the second part of this Conclusion attention is paid to the politics of panic. Finally, in concluding, some brief thoughts are offered about the significance of sociology in these troubling times of immanent but still unusual panic.

Why don't we trust ourselves?

In Chapter 3 attention was paid to the popular psychology of panic. The doubtless sincere concern of the authors and counsellors to help panicking people go about their routine daily lives nevertheless revealed something. The solution to panic attacks is to observe yourself as if from a distance. It is to try to create a split between yourself as a panicking body undergoing certain physical experiences (shortness of breath, perspiration, palpitations and so on), and yourself as an observer immune from these experiences and therefore able to respond to them. But of what does the response consist? It involves the development and use of tools which will subordinate the body to a series of instrumental processes which will gradually bring the body under control and make its actions more or less predictable.

Let's think about the wider message of these kinds of claims. Yes, they might well be highly effective in getting the otherwise panicking person to resume their role in the networks of interdependency,[1] but the fundamental lesson they teach emphasizes taking a distance from yourself. In other words one of the least trustworthy things in the world is yourself, and so you need to become like a mechanic of the self, armed with the right tools to maintain your status as an established participant in the complexity of social life. The popular psychology teaches a lesson about the fragility of the self. The solution is to change the self not the world which makes us fragile. Indeed this world is taken to be inevitable and without alternative. The lesson is, in the first instance, not to trust yourself. The success of popular psychology rather seems to point to the appeal and resonance of the lesson. But why are we untrustworthy to ourselves? If Christopher Lasch is right it's because our social character has been shaped by the demands of mass culture.[2]

Now the motive principle of mass culture is easy to identify. Not to put any fine point on the matter, it's the generation of capitalist profit. This claim has been implicit throughout the book. Moving away from Lasch's terms, the complex networks of interdependency can be identified as the sociological aspects of a system of production needing flexible labour and a system of consumption requiring rapid change and a lack of durable things. Lasch makes a point that echoes to the argument about ontological insecurity and indeed the popular psychology: 'The social arrangements that support a system of mass production and mass consumption tend to discourage initiative and self-reliance and to promote dependence, passivity, and a spectatorial state of mind both at work and play' (Lasch 1984: 27). According to Lasch the mass production introduced in the early twentieth century required predictability on the part of workers. This was achieved through the imposition of scientific management techniques (Fordism) which took initiative away from the worker. The action of labour was broken up into a series of discrete movements which were subjected to instrumental control. Here Lasch is making a historical point, but his insight remains perfectly valid. As Richard Sennett (1999) has shown, technologies and relationships of production in places like contemporary bakeries are designed in terms of systemic predictability at the expense of worker's creativity. It is possible for the consumer to trust in the quality of the loaf which will be much the same today as it was yesterday. The unpredictable, active, human factor has been taken out of the production process. Buying bread has become a routine action which adds its own small dose to the bigger medicine of ontological security. Furthermore, Lasch emphasizes how mass production implies mass consumption and this, in its turn, points to a certain kind of social character. Consumption is only possible and indeed necessary if we have no sense of being sufficient unto ourselves, if we have no sense of an alternative to going shopping. According to Lasch, this is historically specific: 'People had to be discouraged from providing for their own wants and resocialized as consumers. Industrialism by its very nature tends to discourage home production and to make people dependent on the market' (Lasch 1984: 29). This meant teaching lessons in what it means to be a consumer, and what it means is dependency. It means ontological insecurity. For Lasch mass production and mass consumption are similar because: 'both tended to discourage enterprise and independent thinking and to make the individual distrust his own judgement, even in matters of taste' (Lasch 1984: 29). Should I wear my unfashionable coat anymore? It still keeps me warm, but what will people think of me? Would you publicly use a 4-year-old cell phone, even if it were in full working order?

Let me put this claim into different terms. The contemporary networks of interdependency are associated with capitalist relationships of production and consumption. These relationships require workers and consumers who behave predictably and instrumentally. The workers are required to carry out specific tasks with the maximum speed and the minimum of personal idiosyncrasy (in the contemporary office this takes the form of an instrumental notion of 'quality'). The consumers are required to be amenable to changing tastes and, indeed, to feel their social status (their status as established not outsiders, their status as reminders of what we ought to be like and not, as with folk devils, reminders of what we ought not to be) to be linked with how they appear not with who they are, with what they *have*. Once again, the situation is one of ontological insecurity because: 'the repeated experience of uneasy self-scrutiny, of submission to expert judgement, of distrust of their own capacity to make intelligent decisions, either as producers or consumers, colors people's perceptions both of themselves and of the world around them' (Lasch 1984: 29). The situation is exacerbated because the sphere of consumption necessarily lacks durable things in which it is possible to trust. Consumption is only viable as an economic system when the things purchased today are used up today or, if they cannot be used quite so quickly, might be revealed to be inadequate tomorrow. Today's confident purchase is tomorrow's garbage, and so the consumer is given one more reason to lack trust in her or his own ability to make durable judgements and decisions. Advertising creates dependency by intimating the untrustworthiness of one's own previous judgements. By this argument when advertising is aspirational, the aspiration it is selling is ontological security. Consequently it's a lie.

According to Lasch, the upshot of all this is the emergence of a *narcissistic* social character. This is the contemporary form of Dostoevsky's egoist. The minimal self mentioned in Chapter 3 is a narcissist. Narcissism is 'a disposition to see the world as a mirror, more particularly as a projection of one's own fears and desires – not because it makes people grasping and self-assertive but because it makes them weak and dependent' (Lasch 1984: 33). Lasch sees the person as someone who has had all self-trust sucked out by the relationships of production and consumption. The world becomes a mirror in which it is hoped to find something trustworthy. These are people who confront ontological insecurity every time they go to work or to the shops, and who are therefore amenable to panic given a precipitating event. They live in a world that is too complex to understand except when its fragility is revealed. As Lasch put it: 'The consumer feels that he lives in a world that defies practical understanding and control, a world of giant bureaucracies, "information overload", and complex, interlocking technological systems vulnerable to sudden breakdown' (Lasch 1984: 33). This world makes people feel helpless: 'it undermines their confidence in their capacity to understand and shape the world and to provide for their own needs' (Lasch 1984: 33). Mirrors are there to look at, not make. The only way fears and desires can be overcome for the person who is woven in to the networks of interdependency (all of us nowadays) is by means of a flight into the ontological security of the acceptance of things which evidently must be and which can only be questioned at the cost of generating panic.

If all of this seems a little general, it can be brought down to earth by a fleeting yet typical example. In Britain in March 2012 there was the outside possibility of a strike by the drivers of petrol tankers. Had there been a strike, petrol stations would have run dry and people would not have been able to travel. For a variety of contingent political reasons having nothing to do with the possible strike itself a government minister advised everyone to fill up their cars with petrol just in case. The impact of the announcement was quick and massive. Long queues formed at petrol stations as people tried to fill up before the reservoirs ran dry, there were forecourt fights, and the increase in petrol buying helped lift UK retail sales by 1.8 per cent (Stewart 2012). This is a very fine example of panic as defined by Smelser. It was a collective behaviour based on a hysterical belief. The precipitating event was the announcement by the government minister. All the drivers were trying to reach what they had unambiguously been told was the rapidly closing exit of a well-fuelled car by getting to the station first. Established patterns of social behaviour broke down because they discovered they were not first at all, or because they thought some people were taking more fuel than they ought. No one had any confidence in their ability to get by for a day or two without a car.

The petrol panic can be understood through the lens of Lasch's account of the narcissistic self. The people who went to the petrol stations were narcissists for whom the world actually makes little or no sense because it is dominated by technological systems which are immensely fragile and can break down easily. The chance of a petrol strike, and the unambiguous although mendacious advice of a government minister, justified their own fears about the world. Specifically, everything seemed to confirm the sense of ontological insecurity. Consequently there was panic, and a retreat to a personal ontological security as represented by a full tank of petrol. At no point were questions raised about the networks of interdependency. Rather the only concern was to ensure one's own security within it. This concern also and inevitably took the form of a call to institutions to maintain supplies and, if need be, to mobilize the army to drive the tankers. There could be no alternative to petrol on demand.

What politics?

It is worth summing up some of the points made so far in this Conclusion. The definition of panic offered in the Introduction has been built on in order to make a sociological claim. *Panic is a realization of ontological insecurity.* This insecurity is a consequence of the complexity, and therefore the fragility, of the networks of interdependency. As such panic is an immanent quality of contemporary social relationships, but it only breaks out when there is a precipitating event. Panic remains unusual because most of the time the predictability and robustness of institutions and what Giddens calls 'environments of action' generates ontological security. Where there is ontological security there is not panic.

These points make it possible to identify the politics of panic. *Since panic is a realization of ontological insecurity, it implies a political struggle to return to, or to rebuild, the guarantors of ontological security. This is even though these erstwhile guarantors are complicit in the complexity which led to the initial panic.* Put more briefly, this is a politics in which the problem is the alleged solution. It is also a *regressive politics*. What does this mean?

The reference to regression is a gesture towards the work of Theodor Adorno. But it's not a gesture towards his more obviously political writing. Instead what I want to do is take up a theme from Adorno's critical enquiry into popular music and to use it in a way he did not, or at least did not explicitly.

Adorno's views on popular music, and especially popular music in America, are well known. He didn't like it at all and was happy to discuss it with words like 'barbarism' and 'idiocy'. Writers who have not actually read Adorno very closely think he was calling people who like popular music barbarians and idiots. But he was not. Adorno was, instead, trying to say something about the cultural forms foisted on people by the culture industry. He was trying to work out how alert and intelligent men and women can be made to like such mass-produced, humanly vacuous, music as jazz. One part of his argument offered a theory about what he called the *regression of listening*. According to Adorno there is regression when there is an inability on the part of listeners to imagine the possibility of any other kind of music, and most certainly any music that is 'oppositional' (Adorno 1991: 41). Music is not oppositional in the simple sense of protest lyrics but in the sense of its refusal to uphold the conventions and formulae of the mass-produced music promulgated by the culture industry in the search for quick profit by giving people what they have been taught they want (if only because advertising tells them there can be no alternative music to which to listen).

Why does this represent 'regression'? Adorno actually has high aspirations and expectations for us. He believes we are all capable of critical reflection on the world and, through such reflection, we will come to resist the oppression lying at the heart of what we are told is our freedom. For Adorno it is the role of culture to assist in this task of inciting, encouraging and sustaining critical activity. Music, like art, literature, film, sociology, should be unsettling and maybe even frightening. Unfortunately 'official' sociology is not like this at all: 'Never was sociology as bankrupt as it is today with the idea of the doubling of the world' (Adorno and Horkheimer 2011: 1). To put it into the terms of this discussion, culture should be a cause of ontological insecurity precisely in order to make us think critically for ourselves about how we live. Culture ought not to 'double the world' by acting as a mirror, but instead it ought to be critical and opening. The mass-produced music of the culture industry doesn't do this, but the music of Schoenberg and Anton Webern most certainly does. Adorno said their music spreads a 'terror' which 'comes not from their incomprehensibility but from the fact that they are all too correctly understood ... they are called individualists, and yet their work is nothing but a single dialogue with the powers which destroy individuality' (Adorno 1991: 52). This music is rejected because it cuts too close to the quick of our anxieties, and the panic it causes leads to a flight to the safety of music that can be known in advance to be predictably comforting.

Music too can play a part in ontological security, but only by means of a regression. Regression then is assent to dependency in a world that is accepted as the way it is and must be. Regression is the ontological security of the embrace of things as they are. What Adorno said of the audience for regressive music applies more generally to men and women who confront the ontological insecurity borne of the fragility of complex networks of interdependency. Just change the references to production and the product with 'networks of dependency': 'They overcome the feeling of impotence that creeps over them in the face of monopolistic production by identifying themselves with the inescapable product' (Adorno 1991: 42). Panic leads to a re-identification with the networks of interdependency. This re-identification is taken to be valid because the networks, and perhaps more precisely the institutions, which consolidate them, are held to be durable and predictable even in times of chaos. In this way they are doubly 'inescapable'. First of all the networks of interdependency and their institutions are 'inescapable' because they are seen to endure and therefore be without chance or need of an alternative. They are secure. Second they are 'inescapable' because they are the only imaginable safe haven when everything else is fragile. They are security. And indeed the offer of security will be redeemed so long as what the institutions and networks require is embraced and acclaimed.

The politics of panic is regressive in precisely the same way. This can be seen in the hostility that is directed towards folk devils. At a surface level the folk devils are feared because they are dangerous. But something far deeper is going on. The folk devils are also feared because their status as outsiders to the established networks of interdependency reveals a truth which cannot be admitted. *It is possible to live a social life which is outside of the institutionalized routines of predictability.* The folk devils are feared because they demonstrate an alternative to identification with the predictable status quo. Of course this claim does not justify a romanticization of the folk devils. They might not be as dangerous as media amplification invariably implies, but they can still be pretty unpleasant to encounter and rarely do they operate according to a progressive, or maybe *any*, political agenda (where progress is understood as critique and as the opposite to regression). The attitude towards expert knowledge is also regressive, even in times of a catastrophic risk event such as Fukushima. Expert knowledge is treated with suspicion because it reveals the truth of complex technological systems. This is the truth the media disguise when the coverage of risk events becomes increasingly technical, as if it makes sense as a story and not merely as abstract information. In the face of nuclear energy and the like most of us actually and really are completely impotent both in terms of action and understanding. We do not know the difference between a 'plume of smoke' and an 'airborne toxic event', if indeed there really is one. The experts are often impotent too. Social media tell stories of impotence in as much as they say and show what is being done in the wake of the precipitating event. The people who post their panic on Facebook are simply showing the extent to which they are objects who can only understand what is happening by reference to forces *out there*. Yet this impotence is hidden by the act of the self-production of media. It creates a delusion of action. Using a cell phone is not the same as freedom or control over one's own life. Indeed to think it is might well be a massive part of the problem. To this extent social media are not so very different to popular psychology and counselling.

Consequently the institutional politics borne of panic takes the form of claims of an ability to ensure ontological security. But here lies the rub. A politics stressing ontological security only has an appeal in circumstances that are confronted as creating insecurity. As such political campaigns need to play a double game. On the one hand they have to reveal and indeed generate ontological insecurity in order for, on the other hand, the claims about the ability of policies to make things secure to have any impact and appeal. This is exactly the double game that was played by European political leaders (the politicians of institutions and predictability) during the alleged sovereign debt crisis which broke out around 2010. First of all there was the introduction of so-called 'austerity' measures. These were targeted at the dismantling of welfare provision, and therefore they created ontological insecurity. This was because it became impossible to be confident in the state provision of any semblance of a safety-net in the times of need. Smelser might well have gone further and seen in these policies a deliberate creation of panic, since he saw welfare provision as reducing the panic associated with unemployment (Smelser 1962: 135). Yet, second, this creation of insecurity was softened by promises in the ability of these very policies eventually to resolve economic problems and, thereby, generate enough wealth to make sure safety-nets might never be needed ever again. Put another way, the political class created the problems it promised to be able to solve. And within all of this is a threat. If insecurity can be created once, it can be created again and again if you do not accept what is 'necessary'. Such is the arrogance of the contemporary institutional politician. Such too is the extent of regression. Sometimes the politicians are believed and even applauded.[3]

Again what Adorno said of regressive listening applies to regressive politics: 'Underlying it is the knowledge that the security of shelter under the ruling conditions is a provisional one, that it is only a respite, and that eventually everything must collapse' (Adorno 1991: 49). Regressive politics ultimately offers the security of delusion, hubris and self-deceit.

Conclusion

As life becomes more entangled in complex networks of interdependency the possibility and danger of fragility is magnified. When fragility is confronted people rather like us, reactively panic. We do not creatively act because a life lived in the networks of interdependency, especially given the extent to which these networks are implicated in capitalist relationships of production and consumption, makes us lose confidence in ourselves. We do not trust ourselves enough to be able to act. Instead we embrace pretty much anything which promises to be able to rebuild the predictable and robust world of ontological security. This, in brief, is the overall conclusion of the argument developed in this little book. So what?

I think the overall conclusion is helpful because it opens up the possibility of making some observations.

- *First* of all, it is possible to identify the weak spot in contemporary social relationships. The networks of interdependency are at their weakest at precisely the point where they are at their most diverse, ambitious and, it must be said, technologically impressive.
- *Second*, the very institutions and networks upon which contemporary social life depends, and which are the basis of ontological security, contain ontological insecurity as an immanent possibility. This possibility breaks out when there is a precipitating event.
- *Third*, these events are immanent within complex technological systems and established and outsider figurations which are confronting rapid social change. Despite what the focus on moral panics might imply, precipitating events are not primarily social actions.

Fourth, complex networks backed up by institutions imply a social character that is oriented towards predictability and the durable. This is an egoistic and narcissistic social character from which all self-confidence has been leeched. It is a character that confronts itself as an object rather than a subject.

Fifth, all of this means a politics of regression built on the principle of there being no secure – and indeed imaginable – alternative to the way things are now. The only alternative is ontological insecurity, and therefore the chance of an alternative causes panic.

This is where sociology comes in, not with the arrogance of providing an answer, but instead with a concern to encourage thought and maybe even action. Thinking *sociologically* about panic changes the terms of the debate. Panic does not have to be accepted as natural, inevitable, the way things must be. Rather panic can be confronted with a series of questions: Why do we panic? Why do we panic about some things and not others? What benefits from our panic? In other words, raising sociological questions can make us subjects of our panic and, thereby, give us back a degree of control over our lives. Of course none of this is going to stop a nuclear power station from exploding. Nothing will. But in the meantime perhaps we will be able to live more *human* lives and stop worrying about what *might* happen, stop accepting the safe death of regression.

So what is the sociological message about panic? It's simple to state, harder to live. Don't panic about panic. Use panic to live an active human life, not the passive reactive life that institutions and regressive politics advocate. Panic can make us human again. If we work with panic and don't panic about it, we can begin to see where the durable *really* resides.

FURTHER READING, VIEWING AND LISTENING

This little book has been written in the spirit of an invitation to start thinking for ourselves about panic. It's also been written in terms of my commitment to the *sociological imagination* rather than to a discipline called 'sociology' or – even worse – 'social science'. If social life can be understood scientifically it cannot also be a human life, and if knowledge is confined within disciplinary boundaries it cannot possibly get anywhere close to grasping the complexity of what it entails to be human, living in this world with other people. We must draw on anything and everything with the potential to help us understand the links between our private troubles and public issues and, on such a basis, begin to work out what are the wise questions to ask, the wise ways of acting. These are of course rather second-hand thoughts and draw directly from the ever-wonderful, ever-provocative and ever-inspiring position mapped by C. Wright Mills in his 1959 book *The Sociological Imagination*. There are a couple of editions of the book, but whatever edition you use, in the first instance focus on Chapters 1, 10 and the Appendix 'On Intellectual Craftsmanship'. Don't just *read* Mills though. Work with him, think with him, and you will develop the sociological imagination.

Why am I saying this? Well, it has implications for how I envisage the role and content of this guide to further reading. It explains why I've called this section of the book 'Further reading, viewing and listening'. I'm not going to give a list of sources I found useful in formulating the problems in this book but did not explicitly refer to, and neither am I going to provide a list of texts that look as if they could be useful on the basis of a quick Google search. Instead, what I want to do is point towards a range of texts I think might be helpful in stimulating thought about panic. The range is far from encompassing. It offers some points of departure for your own journeys in the practice of a sociological imagination about panic. Thinking sociologically means opening up our horizons, it means thinking beyond sociology as a discipline with its own reading lists validating some sources and condemning others to oblivion. *Doing* sociology usually leads to banality – *thinking* sociologically usually doesn't.

Newspapers and broadcast news

Read a newspaper everyday. I don't mean you should read every page, but keep yourself very aware of what is going on in the world and look at how newspapers report panic. It's always good to read a quality newspaper, but given the concerns of this book it's also a good idea to keep yourself aware of how the tabloid press is reporting other issues too. Remember: the case of Keely Fujiyama says a lot more about media and risk than most academic books on the subject. It's also important to watch television news broadcasts on a regular basis. Watch a range of them to spot continuities and differences in the emergence of moral panics and folk devils.

YouTube

Following on from watching news broadcasts, and indeed as a way of catching broadcasts you have missed, use YouTube. Although YouTube is a bit of a labyrinth full of diversions, its importance as a resource and indeed phenomenon is enormous. Whatever you want, you'll find. But make sure you don't waste time watching clips of people falling over and such like. It's also worth searching YouTube for subjects like 'moral panics'. You'll find some excellent visual material based on, and clarifying, the academic literature.

Books

I have used Don DeLillo's *White Noise*, and I recommend it heartily. It moves across the fields of panic. It's about risk, the media, psychology, metaphysics and is also pretty funny. It is certainly a lot funnier than *The Brothers Karamazov*, but if you want to get to the heart of metaphysical panic you simply must read Dostoevsky's masterpiece. Indeed I'm inclined to go so far as to say you must read Dostoevsky if you want to be a fully functioning human being. DeLillo writes literature speaking directly to the sociological imagination, so once you've read *White Noise*, move out to his other books. Start with *Falling Man*. Published in 2007, *Falling Man* explores the impact of the 9/11 attacks on a lawyer based at the World Trade Center. The book inevitably focuses on the question of terrorism. So did some of DeLillo's earlier novels, most notably *Players* of 1977.

It's important to try – although inevitably we can only fail – to get inside what the nuclear might be about in human terms. Read John Hersey's book *Hiroshima* (which is based on a *New Yorker* article he published in 1946) and Kenzoburō Ōe's *Hiroshima Notes* (published in Japanese in 1965 and in English translation in 1981). Both offer engagement with, and reflection on, the impact on individual people of the atom bombing of the city. Neither book is an easy read although they are both beautifully written – and this is precisely why they *must* be read.

Music

Before or after reading the books by Hersey and Ōe you also need to listen to a piece of music. *Do not under any circumstances* read and listen at the same time and *do not* stop the piece of music short – listen to all of it, and you will begin to feel metaphysical panic. It's Krzysztof Penderecki's *Threnody for the Victims of Hiroshima* (1960). You can find it on YouTube, and you should play it *very* loud, preferably over headphones. Let the music swamp you.

Films

Start with the original version of *Godzilla*. This 1954 film gives a Japanese perspective on the implications of nuclear technology and, if Peter Carey is right, it can be used as a point from which to begin to explore the world of contemporary *manga*.

Metaphysical panic was one of the big themes in European art house cinema. Start with Michelangelo Antonioni's *L'eclisse* of 1962. The end of this film is amazingly poignant, but it only makes sense if you have paid full attention to everything else. But you ought also to watch Bergman's *The Seventh Seal* (1957) and Tarkovsky's incredible 1979 meditation *Stalker* (but make sure you've got a comfortable seat because it *is* long and by Hollywood standards not a lot happens). The nuclear theme can also be found in *The China Syndrome* (1979). Panic caused by the risk of medical technology is the theme of Steven Soderbergh's *Contagion* (2011). Then again, you can also learn a lot about panic from films such as *Airplane!* (1980) and *Snakes on a Plane* (2006). For an exploration of psychological panic against the backdrop of historical events, watch Woody Allen's *Zelig* (1983). For some ideas about what to do when the world is about to end there is *Melancholia*, the 2011 film by Lars von Trier.

Life

Take a flight, wait until you are a few thousand metres up, look out of the window and ask yourself: 'I wonder what would happen if that bit fell off?.'

NOTES

1 Panic and risk

1 However Tokyo is not quite as familiar as Western audiences might like to think. The rubbing of 'real' Tokyo against dream Tokyo was the substance of the joke of the 2003 movie *Lost in Translation*.
2 The film is extremely strongly reminiscent of the tragic story of Mehran Karimi Nasseri, a refugee from Iran who was refused entry to France and lived for 17 years (from 1988 to 2006) in the departure lounge at Charles de Gaulle airport in Paris. The film's publicity however made no mention of Nasseri.
3 The problem with this approach was clearly demonstrated by the British media in 2006, when the H5N1 virus, commonly called bird flu was, allegedly, about to kill everyone. The whole nation became ornithologists and lurid television reports showed dead birds from Asia on English beaches (the symbolism was heavy) surrounded by people in protective clothing. Language, imagery and symbolism all became exhausted. For a discussion of all of this, see Bauman 2010: 79–82.

2 Panic and morality

1 The painting can be seen at: http://www.pallant.org.uk/whats-on/exhibitions/past-exhibitions/2008/colin-self-art-in-the-nuclear-age
2 I am not going to go into detail about the Mods and Rockers. First of all, everything is in Cohen's book and, second, it is now ancient history. Even I have only a slight memory of them. I was brought up near Brighton, and I can vividly remember walking with my father along Brighton promenade, I would have been around 5 years old at the time. A group of loud and to my little eyes huge Rockers walked menacingly towards us. My father took my hand and just said 'walk in a straight line'. We did, the Rockers moved out of our way (I think a few

of them smiled at me), and so ended my only close encounter with one of the great folk devils of the 1960s.

3 Panic and trust

1 There are a number of problems with Giddens's idea of the reflexive project of the self. First, when he says individuals 'more or less' have to engage with the wider world it is hard to know what 'more or less' can possibly mean. Individuals might have to engage differently, and there might well be gatekeepers on engagement, but all of this is about difference of quality not quantity (as the phrase 'more or less' implies). Second, he says the reactions of others are of secondary importance to 'keeping the narrative going' in the project of the self. But contrary to Giddens this self is inescapably involved in the world with others – after all this is the basic insight of sociology – and therefore the reactions of others are drastically important. Third, and most importantly, the idea of the reflexive project of the self is internally contradictory. Reflexivity implies limitless narration and re-narration in order to maintain a sense of the continuous self. In other words the continuous self is known through its changes. Consequently the idea only works if there is something about the self that is bracketed out from reflexivity (there must be a self that reflects on the reflexivity in order to maintain a sense of continuity as a distinctive self). This super-reflexive self is either a metaphysical category or stabilized through its relationships with others. But Giddens doesn't do metaphysics and, as we have seen, relationships with others are of only secondary importance for self-identity.

Conclusion

1 Before anyone thinks I am making snide attacks on something I don't understand, I just want to provide a personal anecdote. I once developed a fear of airports – not flying or planes, but airports (there was a rational reason for this). I was only able to overcome the panic induced by a departure lounge thanks to the use of cognitive tools I developed through a number of effective counselling sessions. The counselling was indeed aimed at giving me a toolbox, and I was encouraged to see myself as a member of a cinema audience watching a film starring me. But I accept this hardly makes me an expert.
2 Of course the phrase 'mass culture' is very unfashionable nowadays, but as with many unfashionable things it remains useful so long as the meaning of the word 'mass' is specified. 'Mass' conventionally has been taken to mean 'all the same', but I want to use the word with a different and simpler inflection as meaning simply 'large scale'.
3 A different but pertinent angle on this politics of regression is in J. G. Ballard's 2006 novel *Kingdom Come*.

REFERENCES

Adorno, Theodor (1991) *The Culture Industry. Selected Essays on Mass Culture*, ed. J.M. Bernstein, London: Routledge.
Adorno, Theodor and Max Horkheimer (2011) *Towards a New Manifesto*, trans. Rodney Livingstone, London: Verso.
Allen, Nick (2011) 'Japan earthquake: the exodus of Tokyo', *Daily Telegraph*, 16 March. http://www.telegraph.co.uk/news/worldnews/asia/japan/8385978/Japan-earthquake-the-exodus-of-Tokyo.html
Ballard, J.G. (2006) *Kingdom Come*, London: Harper.
—— (2008) *Miracles of Life: An Autobiography*, London: Fourth Estate.
Batty, David (2010) 'Icelandic volcano now appears to be dormant, say scientists', *The Guardian*, 23 May. http://www.guardian.co.uk/world/2010/may/23/iceland-volcano-minimal-eruption-activity
Bauman, Zygmunt (1990) *Thinking Sociologically*, Oxford: Blackwell.
—— (2006) *Liquid Fear*, Cambridge: Polity.
—— (2010) *44 Letters from the Liquid Modern World*, Cambridge: Polity.
Beck, Ulrich (1992) *Risk Society: Towards a New Modernity*, trans. Mark Ritter, London: Sage.
Becker, Howard (1963) *Outsiders: Studies in the Sociology of Deviance*, New York: Free Press.
Benjamin, Walter (1973) *Illuminations*, trans. Harry Zohn, London: Fontana.
British Council of Churches (1946) *The Era of Atomic Power: Report of a Commission Appointed by the British Council of Churches*, London: SCM Press.
Carey, Peter (2005) *Wrong About Japan*, London: Faber & Faber.
Cohen, Stanley (2002) *Folk Devils and Moral Panics: The Creation of Mods and Rockers*, third edition, London: Routledge.
—— (2011) 'Whose side are we on? The undeclared politics of moral panic theory', *Crime, Media, Culture*, 7(3): 237–43.
Daily Mail (2009) 'The whole body airport scanner that reveals your underwear', 31 March. http://www.dailymail.co.uk/sciencetech/article-1166157/The-body-airport-scanner-reveals-underwear.html

DeLillo, Don (1986) *White Noise*, London: Picador.
Dostoevsky, Fyodor (1992) *The Brothers Karamazov*, trans. Richard Pevear and Larissa Volokhonsky, New York: Alfred A. Knopf.
Durkheim, Emile (1984) *The Division of Labour in Society*, new edition, trans. W.D. Hall, London: Macmillan.
Elias, Norbert (1978) *What is Sociology?* London: Hutchinson.
Elias, Norbert and John Scotson (1994) *The Established and the Outsiders: A Sociological Enquiry into Community Problems*, second edition, London: Sage.
Fejes, Fred (2000) '"Murder, perversion and moral panic: the 1954 media campaign against Miami's homosexuals and the discourse of civic betterment', *Journal of the History of Sexuality*, 9(3): 305–47.
Fraher, Amy L. (2004) '"Flying the friendly skies": why US commercial airline pilots want to carry guns', *Human Relations*, 57(5): 573–95.
Giddens, Anthony (1990) *The Consequences of Modernity*, Stanford, CA: Stanford University Press.
—— (1991) *Modernity and Self-Identity: Self and Society in the Late Modern Age*, Cambridge: Polity.
—— (1994) *Beyond Left and Right. The Future of Radical Politics*, Cambridge: Polity.
—— (2009) *The Politics of Climate Change*, Cambridge: Polity.
Gigerenzer, Gerd (2004) 'Dread risk, September 11, and fatal traffic accidents', *Psychological Science*, 15(4): 286–7.
Gilligan, Andrew (2011) 'Japan earthquake: residents flee as quake fears spread', *Daily Telegraph*, 15 March. http://www.telegraph.co.uk/news/worldnews/asia/japan/8383978/Japan-earthquake-residents-flee-as-quake-fears-spread.html
Habermas, Jürgen (1989) *The Structural Transformation of the Public Sphere: An Inquiry into a Category of Bourgeois Society*, trans. Thomas Burger, Cambridge, MA: MIT Press.
Hall, Stuart, Chas Critcher, Tony Jefferson, John Clarke and Brian Roberts (1979) *Policing the Crisis: Mugging, the State and Law and Order*, London: Macmillan.
Hunt, Arnold (1997) '"Moral panic" and moral language in the media', *British Journal of Sociology*, 48(4): 629–48.
Ingham, Charlotte (2000) *Panic Attacks: What They Are, Why They Happen, and What You Can Do about Them*, London: Thorsons.
Kormos, Theresa C. (2003) 'Behavioral treatment for fear of flying', *Journal of the American Psychiatric Nurses Association*, 9(5): 145–50.
Kynaston, David (2007) *Austerity Britain, 1945–51*, London: Bloomsbury.
Lasch, Christopher (1979) *The Culture of Narcissism: American Life in an Age of Diminishing Expectations*, New York: W.W. Norton.
—— (1984) *The Minimal Self: Psychic Survival in Troubled Times*, New York: W.W. Norton.
McCurry, Justin (2011) 'Radiation fears prompt Tokyo exodus', *The Guardian*, 15 March. http://www.guardian.co.uk/world/2011/mar/15/radiation-tokyo-flights-cancelled?INTCMP=SRCH

McCurry, Justin and Robert Booth (2011) 'Britain joins countries urging their citizens to leave Tokyo', *The Guardian*, 16 March. http://www.guardian.co.uk/world/2011/mar/16/britain-urging-citizens-leave-tokyo?INTCMP=SRCH

McRobbie, Angela and Sarah Thornton (1995) 'Rethinking "moral panic" for multi-mediated social worlds', *British Journal of Sociology*, 46(4): 559–74.

Meikle, James (2012) 'Ryanair passengers tell of terrifying descent over the Alps', *The Guardian*, 6 April. http://www.guardian.co.uk/business/2012/apr/06/ryanair-terrifying-descent-over-alps?INTCMP=SRCH

Moeller, Susan D. (1999) *Compassion Fatigue: How the Media Sell Disease, Famine, War and Death*, New York: Routledge.

Newgent, Rebecca A., Derrick A. Paladino and Cynthia A. Reynolds (2006) 'Single session treatment of non-traumatic fear of flying with eye-movement desensitization reprocessing: pre and post September 11', *Clinical Case Studies*, 5(1): 25–36.

Oremus, Will (2011) 'Are people still afraid to fly on 9/11?', *Slate*, 9 September. http://www.slate.com/articles/news_and_politics/explainer/2011/09/are_people_still_afraid_to_fly_on_911.html

Poynting, Scott, Greg Noble and Paul Tabar (2001) 'Middle Eastern appearances: "ethnic gangs", moral panic and media framing', *Australian and New Zealand Journal of Criminology*, 34(1): 67–90.

Qian, Yanfeng (2010) 'Shanghai pollution reaches a new high', *China Daily*, 25 November. http://www.chinadaily.com.cn/china/2010–11/25/content_11604770.htm

Quarantelli, E.L. (2001) *The Sociology of Panic*, Preliminary Paper 283, University of Delaware Disaster Research Centre.

Rieff, Philip (1960) *Freud: The Mind of the Moralist*, London: Victor Gollancz.

Rohloff, Amanda (2011) 'Extending the concept of moral panic: Elias, climate change and civilization', *Sociology*, 45(4): 634–49.

Sennett, Richard (1999) *The Corrosion of Character: Personal Consequences of Work in the New Capitalism*, New York: W.W. Norton.

Shields, Rob (1991) *Places on the Margin: Alternative Geographies of Modernity*, London: Routledge.

Simmel, Georg (1990) *The Philosophy of Money*, second edition, trans. Tom Bottomore and David Frisby, London: Routledge.

Sinn, Hans-Werner (2012) *The Green Paradox: A Supply-Side Approach to Global Warming*, Cambridge, MA: MIT Press.

Smelser, Neil J. (1962) *Theory of Collective Behavior*, London: Routledge & Kegan Paul.

Stern, Lord Nicholas (2006) *Stern Review on the Economics of Climate Change*, London: HMSO.

Stewart, Heather (2012) 'UK retail sales boosted by petrol panic buying', *The Guardian*, 20 April. http://www.guardian.co.uk/business/2012/apr/20/uk-retail-sales-petrol-panic-buying

tsunami disaster (Japan, 2011) 6, 14–15, 31
Tubridy, Áine 80–6
Tucker, Miriam 77

United 93 (film) 7

von Trier, Lars 110

Waddington, P.A.J. 56

Weber, Max 69–73
Webern, Anton 102
Wheeler, Virginia 32
Williams, Rowan 36–7

Yoshida, Masashi 19
Young, Jock 51
YouTube 109

Zelig (film) 110

tsunami disaster (Japan, 2011) 6, 14–15, 31
Tubridy, Áine 80–6
Tucker, Miriam 77

United 93 (film) 7

von Trier, Lars 110

Waddington, P.A.J. 56

Weber, Max 69–73
Webern, Anton 102
Wheeler, Virginia 32
Williams, Rowan 36–7

Yoshida, Masashi 19
Young, Jock 51
YouTube 109

Zelig (film) 110

Taylor & Francis

eBooks

FOR LIBRARIES

ORDER YOUR FREE 30 DAY INSTITUTIONAL TRIAL TODAY!

Over 22,000 eBook titles in the Humanities, Social Sciences, STM and Law from some of the world's leading imprints.

Choose from a range of subject packages or create your own!

Benefits for you

- Free MARC records
- COUNTER-compliant usage statistics
- Flexible purchase and pricing options

Benefits for your user

- Off-site, anytime access via Athens or referring URL
- Print or copy pages or chapters
- Full content search
- Bookmark, highlight and annotate text
- Access to thousands of pages of quality research at the click of a button

For more information, pricing enquiries or to order a free trial, contact your local online sales team.

UK and Rest of World: **online.sales@tandf.co.uk**

US, Canada and Latin America:
e-reference@taylorandfrancis.com

www.ebooksubscriptions.com

ALPSP Award for BEST eBOOK PUBLISHER 2009 Finalist

Taylor & Francis eBooks
Taylor & Francis Group

A flexible and dynamic resource for teaching, learning and research.

Stoller, Gary (2006) 'Fear of flying can cripple workers', *USA Today*, 20 March. http://www.usatoday.com/travel/flights/2006-03-20-fear-of-flying-usat_x.htm

Tubridy, Áine (2003) *When Panic Attacks*, Dublin: Gill and Macmillan.

Tucker, Mirian E. (2001) 'Fear of flying after 9/11', *Pittsburgh Post-Gazette*, 6 December. http://miriametucker.com/Fear_of_Flying_After_9_11.html

Waddington, P.A.J. (1986) 'Mugging as a moral panic: a question of proportion', *British Journal of Sociology*, 37(2): 245–59.

Weber, Max (1948) *From Max Weber: Essays in Sociology*, ed. and trans. Hans H. Gerth and C. Wright Mills, London: Routledge & Kegan Paul.

Wheeler, Virginia (2011) 'Starving Brit Keely: my nightmare trapped in city of ghosts – Tokyo', *The Sun*, 17 March. http://www.thesun.co.uk/sol/homepage/news/3473142/My-nightmare-trapped-in-post-tsunami-Tokyo-City-of-Ghosts.html

Williams, Rowan (2000) *Christ on Trial: How the Gospel Unsettles Our Judgement*, London: HarperCollins.

Wimmer, Jeffrey, and Thorsten Quandt (2006) 'Living in the risk society', *Journalism Studies*, 7(2): 336–47.

Young, Jock (2011) 'Moral panics and the transgressive other', *Crime, Media, Culture*, 7(3): 245–58.

INDEX

Adorno, Theodor 100–5
advertising 98
African-Caribbean men 55–6
airline crews 75–6
Airplane! (film) 110
Allen, Nick 16, 19
Allen, Woody 110
American Psychiatric Association
  Diagnostic and Statistical Manual of Mental Disorders 78
anti-social behaviour orders 54
Antonioni, Michelangelo 56–7, 110
Australia 62–3

Ballard, J.G. 22
banking crisis (from 2008) 5–6
Bauman, Zygmunt 2–3, 10
Beck, Ulrich 22–34, 37, 39–40, 63–4, 69, 94
Becker, Howard 55, 59
Benjamin, Walter 38, 92
Bergman, Ingmar 56, 110
Birmingham Centre for Contemporary Cultural Studies 55
Brighton 61
British Council of Churches 40–7, 49–51

capitalism 97
Carey, Peter 20, 110
character traits 18
Chernobyl accident (1986) 20–1, 30
The China Syndrome (film) 110
climate change 23–5, 91
Cohen, Stanley 5, 12, 52–61
cohesion, social 60
collective nature of panic behaviour 4–5, 35
'compassion fatigue' 30–32
complexity of social relationships 4, 8–9, 74, 92, 100
computer viruses 1–3
Contagion (film) 110
contraception 46
cultural studies 56
culture, role of 101–2

DeLillo, Don 65–70, 75, 81, 84–5, 109
'deviant' groups 51–4, 59–60
division of labour 8
Dostoevsky, Fyodor 42–4, 57, 87–8, 98, 109
Durkheim, Émile 8

L'eclisse (film) 110
egoism 43–5, 87, 98, 106
Elias, Norbert 9–10, 58–64
energy industry 44
expert systems 34, 71, 74, 84
experts, trust in 35, 74, 103
Eyjafjallajökull eruption (2010) 11

family relationships 47
'fascination', different meanings of 28–30, 33
fear 2–3; as distinct from panic 12; of flying 71, 74–81, 86–7
Fejes, Fred 48–51
figurations (Elias) 9–10
films about panic 19–21, 56–7, 77, 110
flight in response to panic 4–7, 17–19, 91
folk devils 11, 46, 56–64, 90, 94, 97, 103
fragility of social relationships 4, 10–12, 35, 47, 50, 57–8, 61, 74, 88, 90, 92, 94, 100, 102
Fraher, Amy L. 75–7, 80
Fujiyama, Keely 31–3, 36, 108
Fukushima accident (2011) 14–19, 20–2, 30–7, 68–70, 90, 94, 103

Giddens, Anthony (and 'Giddens paradox') 23, 71–5, 80–6, 93, 100
Gilligan, Andrew 15, 17, 19, 34–5
global warming 23–4; *see also* climate change
Godzilla (film) 21, 110
Greene, Graham 61
greenhouse gases 21, 24
'group charisma' 60–1, 64

Habermas, Jürgen 29
Hall, Stuart 55
Hersey, John 109

Hiroshima 40–2, 68
homosexuality 48–9
Hunt, Arnold 51
Hurricane Katrina 69
hysteria 7, 99

Ingham, Christine 81–4
institutions, instrumentality of 94
interdependency, networks of 8–12, 18, 27–8, 35, 37, 45–52, 57–64, 67, 74, 78, 92–105; exclusion from 63–4

Japanese culture 21

Kant, Immanuel 25
Kormos, Theresa C. 79
Kynaston, David 47

Lasch, Christopher 85–8, 94–9

Mace, David 47
Mass Observation 47
mass production and mass consumption 96–7
media influences 5, 19–20, 26–38, 45–9, 53–8, 66–8, 91–2, 103
Melancholia (film) 110
metaphysical panic 42–5, 56, 68–70, 94, 109–10
Miami 48–9
Millennium Bug 1–2
Mills, C. Wright 107–8
Mods and Rockers 52, 61
Moeller, Susan 30–2
money, trust in 71, 93
moral entrepreneurs 55, 59
moral panic 45–8, 50–62, 90–1; definition of 53
morality, meaning of 50–1
motoring accidents 89
mugging 55–6
music 100–2

mutual dependency 10; *see also* interdependency, networks of

Nagasaki 40–2, 68
narcissistic social character 98–9, 106
natural disasters 4, 11
New Orleans 69
Newgent, Rebecca 78–9
news media 108
'9/11' attacks 37, 74–9, 88–9, 109
nuclear technology, development of 40–2

Ōe, Kenzoburō 109–10
ontological security 74, 76–9, 92–105; four strands in 92–4
Otherness 63
'outsider' status 58–64, 90, 94, 103

panic: cultural context of 17–18, 20; definitions of 3–8, 11–12, 16–17, 74, 93, 100; as distinct from fear 12; popular psychology literature on 80–1, 83–4, 86, 95–6
panic attacks 78, 81–3, 95
Parsons, Talcott 7
Penderecki, Krzysztof 110
politics 39; of panic 100, 103–4
pollution 23–4
power struggles within society 61
Poynting, Scott 61–3
precipitating events 16–17, 19, 54, 68, 93, 99–100, 105
predictability 93, 106
public sphere 29, 33

Quarantelli, E.L. 7

recklessness 41, 44, 46, 52
reflexive project of the self 82–4

regression (Adorno) 100–5
Rieff, Philip 87
risk, definition of 21–2
risk events 12, 91, 94, 103
risk society theory 20–26, 35, 39, 65, 69

Schoenberg, Arnold 102
scientific management techniques 96
scientific rationality 25–6
Scotson, John 58–60
Self, Colin 42–7, 56, 64, 94
self-identity 82–9
Sennett, Richard 96
The Seventh Seal (film) 110
sexual relationships 46–50
Shanghai 22–3
Simmel, Georg 72, 93
Sinn, Hans-Werner 44
Smelser, Neil 4–8, 16–18, 54, 66–8, 91–93, 99, 104
Snakes on a Plane (film) 110
social change 52, 61–2
social media 33–9, 70, 103–4
sociology and sociological thinking, role of 106, 108
Soderbergh, Steven 110
sovereign debt crisis 104
Spielberg, Steven 19
Spirit Airlines 77
Stalker (film) 110
Stern Review (2006) 24–6
The Sun 31

tanker drivers' strike threat (2012) 99–100
Tarkovsky, Andrei 110
teenagers 52
The Terminal (film) 19
trust: breakdown of 71–2, 90–1; definition of 72–4; in experts 34; in institutions 94; in ourselves 95–100